S. HRG. 113–623

U.S. SECURITY IMPLICATIONS OF INTERNATIONAL ENERGY AND CLIMATE POLICIES AND ISSUES

HEARING

BEFORE THE

SUBCOMMITTEE ON INTERNATIONAL
DEVELOPMENT AND FOREIGN ASSISTANCE,
ECONOMIC AFFAIRS, INTERNATIONAL
ENVIRONMENTAL PROTECTION,
AND PEACE CORPS

OF THE

COMMITTEE ON FOREIGN RELATIONS
UNITED STATES SENATE

ONE HUNDRED THIRTEENTH CONGRESS

SECOND SESSION

JULY 22, 2014

Printed for the use of the Committee on Foreign Relations

Available via the World Wide Web: http://www.gpo.gov/fdsys/

U.S. GOVERNMENT PUBLISHING OFFICE

94–134 PDF   WASHINGTON : 2015

CONTENTS

U.S. SECURITY IMPLICATIONS OF INTERNATIONAL ENERGY AND CLIMATE POLICIES AND ISSUES

TUESDAY, JULY 22, 2014

U.S. SENATE, SUBCOMMITTEE ON INTERNATIONAL DEVELOPMENT AND FOREIGN ASSISTANCE, ECONOMIC AFFAIRS, INTERNATIONAL ENVIRONMENTAL PROTECTION, AND PEACE CORPS, COMMITTEE ON FOREIGN RELATIONS,

Washington, DC.

The subcommittee met, pursuant to notice, at 3:11 p.m., in room SD–419, Dirksen Senate Office Building, Hon. Edward J. Markey (chairman of the subcommittee) presiding.

Present: Senators Markey, Murphy, and Barrasso.

OPENING STATEMENT OF HON. EDWARD J. MARKEY, U.S. SENATOR FROM MASSACHUSETTS

Senator MARKEY. Welcome to this very important hearing and we thank all of you for being here. Right now dozens of wars and conflicts dot our world map, from the Sudanese desert to America's longest war in Afghanistan. The root causes of war are diverse and rarely simple, from religious divisions to democratic yearnings. But two major factors have emerged in the modern era that act to strain the strands of stability until they snap—climate change and energy security.

In two regions of our world, climate and energy have recently played major roles in exacerbating what were already tense times. In December 2010, a Tunisian street food vendor lit himself on fire in protest of government corruption and extreme poverty. That spark spread in Tunisia and ignited the Arab Spring.

Yet, feeding this anger over years of corruption and autocratic rule was a more immediate hunger. In 2010, terrible droughts in Russia, in China, and floods in Pakistan decimated wheat harvests and created a global shortage. The price of wheat increased dramatically. The Middle East, home to the world's top nine wheat importers, felt it acutely, especially since the region's farmers struggled with their own parched fields. Much of Syria was gripped with the worst drought it had ever experienced. The price of bread skyrocketed across the region and demands for regime change were not far behind.

About 600 miles north of the Syrian border, the ashes of Malaysia Airline Flight 17 blanket a wheat field in pro-Russia separatist-controlled eastern Ukraine. A surface-to-air missile apparently split the plane and snatched nearly 300 lives. But another weapon has already been deployed in the Russian-Ukraine conflict and in wars across the globe—energy. Russia has already shut off the natural gas spigots to Ukraine. That is more than half of Ukraine's gas supply gone. When winter arrives and natural gas demand spikes, this could become another political and humanitarian crisis, bringing suffering to Ukrainian families and challenges to the new government. Because of Europe's reliance on Russian gas, Putin's energy weapon gives him unparalleled leverage to continue his bullying tactics.

Energy profits can also inflict damage. ISIS, the rebel group destabilizing Iraq, was funded initially by Sunni oil sheiks. ISIS is no longer an upstart insurgency. They are a legitimate threat, consolidating their power around energy holdings as much as sectarian alliances. They have captured Iraqi oil fields. They control much of Syrian oil production, and now they are selling this oil on the black market. Revenues from these operations buy them credibility, weapons, and loyalty—valuable commodities for building a so-called ''caliphate'' in this volatile region.

Since the Industrial Revolution, our world has burned fossil fuels, increasing temperatures and destabilizing our climate. Since that time, we have become more dependent on these same fuels that have destabilized countries and drawn America into international conflicts.

Tunisia is not the first time famine has played a role in a regional conflict. In a 2007 congressional hearing of mine, one general told the story of Somalia, how drought had caused famine, famine had encouraged conflict, how U.S. military forces were sent to ensure food reached those people who needed it and was not used by warlords to gain further power, and how 18 U.S. soldiers lost their lives in what we now call Blackhawk Down. The general believed all went back to the drought that led to the famine.

Russia is not the first country to use energy as a weapon in geopolitics. Much has changed in the U.S. energy sector since OPEC's devastating embargo four decades ago. The shale revolution has boosted U.S. oil production to record levels. Yet much remains the same. Oil still commands a monopoly over our transportation sector. We remain dependent on foreign suppliers to meet nearly one-third of our needs, roughly the same share as 1975, when we banned the export of American oil.

Today we have two panels of experts to help us examine how the twin challenges of climate change and energy security are driving conflicts now and what new conflagrations could be on the horizon. We must do everything in our power today to mitigate the threats that will require military intervention tomorrow. If we fail in our responsibility, it is our men and our women in uniform that will get called upon to try to clean up the mess.

Now I turn to recognize the ranking member of the subcommittee, the Senator from Wyoming, Senator Barrasso.

OPENING STATEMENT OF HON. JOHN BARRASSO, U.S. SENATOR FROM WYOMING

Senator BARRASSO. Thank you very much, Mr. Chairman. Mr. Chairman, the United States is facing serious national security threats across the globe. Americans understand the real direct threats to our national security—aggressive regimes in Syria, Russia, and North Korea, Iran's nuclear weapons program, expanding terrorist threats from al-Qaeda, ISIS, and Hamas, and the unfolding emergency at our borders.

Despite the fact that the administration's foreign policies have led to a more unstable and more dangerous world, the White House last week said that the administration has, ''substantially improved the tranquility of the global community.'' In the face of a growing number of global disasters, Secretary of State Kerry believes that climate change is one of the greatest threats facing our Nation. Secretary Kerry has called climate change the world's most fearsome weapon of mass destruction.

While the rest of the world is looking to the United States to focus and lead on multiple threats to our security, to their security and to ours, as terrorists wage war, as a resurgent Russia invades its neighbors, as commercial airlines are shot down in cold blood, the administration is focused on climate change. Why? Because, according to the White House, the world is tranquil.

The world is far from safe, far from save to preserve our national security. To preserve our national security, we need to spend taxpayer dollars where they are needed the most. Unfortunately, the Obama administration spent $7.5 billion in scarce U.S. taxpayer funds, funds that could have been used to fight terrorism and aggression in the Middle East or in Eastern Europe, to support international climate change programs between fiscal year 2010 and 2012. Folks in my home State of Wyoming would call this spending wasteful and irresponsible at best, especially as our friends and allies struggle with violent, deadly crises that have real implications for our security.

I believe taxpayer money would be better spent improving the security of U.S. embassies, protecting our servicemembers who are serving this Nation in often dangerous locations across the globe, and fighting terrorism and bad actors that wish to do us harm.

The U.S. share of the world's carbon emission has been declining for nearly a decade before President Obama took office. Meanwhile, China's emissions grew by 173 percent from 1998 to 2011 and shows no end in sight.

The drastic steps President Obama wants to take and the damage it will do to our economy would have no impact on global temperatures. That is, unless the President can convince other countries that their economies should stop growing, too. Given the President's current foreign policy record, the chances of that happening are slim.

Countries are starting to realize these policies are hurting their economies and their competitiveness, while yielding few environmental benefits. European Union countries like Germany are abandoning restrictive energy policies in favor of reliable fossil fuels like coal. Just last week, Australia repealed their carbon tax and plans for an emissions trading scheme. Prime Minister Abbott called the carbon tax ''a $9 billion hand brake on our economy.'' He also called it ''a useless, destructive tax'' which damaged jobs, which hurt families' cost of living, and did not actually help the environment.

If President Obama cannot succeed in Paris, all he will have accomplished with his climate change policies will be to have pulled the hand brake on the American economy. He will have no environmental or security benefit to show for it.

This hearing is entitled the ''U.S. Security Implications of International Energy and Climate Policies and Issues.'' I am here to tell you there are serious implications of this administration's energy and climate policies. They have an implication on our economy well-being and most especially on our national security. These policies, already adopted in Europe, have led to crime and to poverty. They have weakened our allies and they will weaken us.

What is needed is an ''all of the above'' energy strategy that creates American jobs, grows our economy, and strengthens our national security. Energy security, not restrictions, will provide the peace and tranquility the global community wants and our Nation deserves.

Thank you, Mr. Chairman. I look forward to the testimony.

Senator MARKEY. I thank the gentleman, and we will turn to our panel. We will hear first from Dr. Daniel Chiu, Deputy Assistant Secretary of Defense for Strategy and Force Development, from the U.S. Department of Defense. We welcome you, doctor. Whenever you are ready, please begin.

STATEMENT OF DANIEL Y. CHIU, PH.D., DEPUTY ASSISTANT SECRETARY OF DEFENSE FOR STRATEGY AND FORCE DEVELOPMENT, U.S. DEPARTMENT OF DEFENSE, WASHINGTON, DC

Dr. CHIU. Thank you, Chairman Markey and Ranking Member Barrasso. Thank you for this opportunity to testify before you today on how DOD is considering the implications of climate change on national security in our war to protect the Nation both in the near and the longer terms.

As you know, the Department of Defense's primary responsibility is to protect our national security interests around the world. To do this, we need to consider all aspects of the global security environment and plan appropriately for the range of potential challenges and prepare for the possibility of unexpected developments, both in the near and long terms.

It is in this context that the Department of Defense must consider a wide range of global trends, to include the effects of climate change, such as sea level rise, shifting climate zones, and more severe weather events, and how these effects could impact our national security. Some of these effects are already being seen today on military bases, installations, and other DOD infrastructure, such as increased flooding from sea level rise and storm surge. We are also seeing the potential for decreased capacity of DOD properties to support training, as well as implications for our supply chains, for the requirements in terms of equipments, vehicles, weapons systems, and other assets that the Department buys.

As a result, we have already found the need to adapt much of our infrastructure, including, for example, building more wind-resistant structures, protecting water supplies, and improving fire breaks at DOD installations. DOD is currently conducting a baseline study, to be completed later this year, to identify what infrastructure is vulnerable to extreme weather events and sea level rise, so that we can ensure that these challenges are addressed appropriately.

In the longer term, the impacts of climate change may have an effect on, and alter, the environments in which our military will be operating. For example, sea level rise may lead us to rethink where and when executing amphibious operations may be appropriate, while changing temperatures and changes in seasonal patterns could impact our assumptions about when and where military operations—certain types of military operations—can take place.

The effects of climate change may also compound instability in other countries and regions by affecting things like the availability of food, water, by instigating human migration and competition for natural resources. This could create significant instabilities and potentially provide an avenue for extremist ideologies and conditions that could foster terrorism or other challenges to U.S. national security.

Therefore, as a Department we are working to better understand how these impacts of climate change can affect our planning and operations in the United States and abroad. We are currently working to take into consideration the impacts of climate change in, for example, our longer term planning scenarios. We are thinking about how the effects of climate change may affect the frequency or severity of events that might lead to the need for humanitarian assistance and disaster relief activities over time. We are looking at our efforts to plan and enhance the capacity of partner militaries to respond to natural disasters, to enable them to effect these operations.

We are also working to address the implications for potentially higher demands for defense support to U.S. civil authorities due to extreme weather events in the United States. The effects of climate change are particularly clear in the Arctic region, where diminishing sea ice will make the Arctic Oceans increasingly accessible. This is a decades-long dynamic, but we must monitor and account for it today. This is why Secretary Hagel released the Department of Defense's Arctic Strategy in November of 2013, which, in support of the National Arctic Strategy released earlier in 2013, seeks through U.S. leadership and collaboration to preserve an Arctic region that remains free of military conflict, in which nations act responsibly and cooperatively, and where economic and energy resources are developed in a safe and sustainable manner.

In order to do so, DOD will focus on ensuring security, support, and safety, promoting defense cooperation, and preparing for a wide range of challenges and contingencies that includes consideration of Arctic contingencies. We do this in the meantime by maintaining domain awareness to ensure that we are prepared for any changes in either Arctic conditions or activities in the Arctic.

The Department currently assesses that the Arctic is a relatively low military threat environment and that existing and planned DOD infrastructure and capabilities in the region are adequate to meet U.S. defense needs in the near and mid-term futures. We will of course continue to reevaluate capabilities and requirements as conditions and regional activities change and will be prepared to address any changes or gaps that could emerge.

Given the nature of climate change, in particular in the Arctic, the United States response to these challenges requires a whole-of-government approach, as well as international collaboration, both of which are the bedrock of our efforts in these areas. By taking a proactive approach to assessment, analysis, and adaptation, DOD believes it can manage the risks posed by the impacts of climate change and minimize the effects to the Department's missions, while continuing to protect national security interests around the world through strong leadership.

Thank you again for this opportunity to speak and I look forward to answering your questions.

[The prepared statement of Dr. Chiu follows:]

PREPARED STATEMENT OF DR. DANIEL Y. CHIU

INTRODUCTION

The Department of Defense (DOD)'s primary responsibility is to protect our Nation's security interests around the world. This includes building security globally through assurance of allies, engagement with partners, and deterrence of adversaries; prevailing in conflicts should they arise; and supporting civil authorities and others around the world in times of emergency. To ensure DOD is adequately prepared to accomplish our missions, we need to consider all aspects of the global security environment and plan appropriately for potential contingencies and the possibility of unexpected developments in both the near and longer terms.

As such, the Department tracks, analyzes, and considers a range of current and future trends and changes, including political-military, economics, demographics, technology, and the environment. All of these issue areas have the potential to significantly impact U.S. national security interests in both positive and negative ways. DOD must take into account these trends to ensure we are able to create and pursue opportunities when they serve our national interests and that we are ready for a wide range of challenges now and into the future.

This is why climate change is included in the 2014 Quadrennial Defense Review. In particular, we noted that: "The impacts of climate change may increase the frequency, scale, and complexity of future missions, including defense support to civil authorities, while at the same time undermining the capacity of our domestic installations to support training activities." The effects of climate change—such as sea-level rise, shifting climate zones, and more severe weather events—will have an impact on our bases and installations at home and overseas; on the operating environment for our troops, ships, and aircraft; and on the global security environment itself as climate change affects other countries around the world.

While all projections contain a degree of uncertainty, the Department considers risk across a wide spectrum of possibilities to ensure DOD is appropriately prepared for the range of possible contingencies. In considering the effects of climate change, scientific data and studies are used to further refine projections and planning. The Department also continues to update and assess this work to ensure that changes are taken into consideration so that plans and capabilities can be adapted, when needed.

NEAR TERM: INFRASTRUCTURE, TRAINING, AND TESTING

The National Climate Assessment, released by the White House earlier this month, noted that the world's climate is already rapidly changing. Certain types of weather events are already occurring more frequently and intensely, including heat waves, heavy downpours, hurricanes, floods, and droughts. Glaciers and Arctic sea ice are melting at a relatively rapid rate, sea levels are rising, and oceans are becoming warmer and more acidic. Moreover, scientists predict that some of these changes will increase in frequency, duration, and intensity over the next 100 years.

Some of these current effects of climate change are being seen on the military bases, installations, and other infrastructure that DOD manages. Our infrastructure serves as the staging platform for the Department's national defense and humanitarian missions, and the natural landscape supports military combat readiness by providing realistic combat conditions and vital resources to personnel. For example, an installation may need a forest or desert landscape for maneuvers, coastal waters for amphibious assault training, or wetlands to prevent flooding and erosion. The effects of climate change will have serious implications for the Department's ability to maintain both its infrastructure and the landscape around it, and to ensure military readiness in the future.

Our coastal installations are already experiencing increased flooding and damage from sea-level rise and increased storm surge; longer term impacts could include increased inundation and erosion. Rising temperature and extreme weather will increase building heating and cooling demand, raising installation energy requirements and operating costs. Those conditions will also increase maintenance requirements for runways and roads, as well as cause disruption to, and competition for, reliable energy and fresh water supplies. Thawing permafrost and melting sea ice are damaging our infrastructure in Alaska and the Arctic region. Changed disease vector distribution, particularly exposure to diseases in regions in which they are not routinely encountered, will increase the complexity and cost of on-going disease management efforts, and may have acute and long-term impacts on personnel health and safety.

The Department also needs to be able to train our forces to meet the evolving nature of the operational environment by training in the field environment to achieve and sustain proficiency in mission requirements. The Department conducts testing in the field environment in anticipation of the military's use of weapons, equipment, munitions, systems, or their components. As such, access to the land, air, and sea space that replicate the operational environment for training and testing is critical to the readiness of the Force.

The impacts of climate change may decrease the capacity of DOD properties to support current testing and training rotation types or levels. Some training and testing lands may lose their carrying capacity altogether. Rising temperatures could lead to an increased number of ''black flag'' (suspended outdoor training) or fire hazard days. Increased dust generation during training activities may interfere with sensitive equipment, resulting in greater repairs, or may require more extensive dust control measures to meet environmental compliance requirements. These conditions could also lead to increased health and safety risks to the Department's personnel.

Climate change also impacts may affect the supplies, equipment, vehicles, and weapons systems the Department buys, where and from whom we buy them, how they are transported and distributed, and how and where they are stockpiled and stored. Changes to the operating environment may require changes to operational parameters for current and planned weapons and equipment, resulting in increased associated maintenance requirements or requirements for new equipment.

Environmental changes may introduce supply-chain vulnerabilities, reducing the availability of, or access to, the materials, resources, and industrial infrastructure needed to manufacture the Department's weapon systems and supplies. They may also cause the interruption of shipment, delivery, or storage and stockpile of materials or manufactured equipment and supplies. Many major corporations have recognized the potential effects of climate change on their operations and are aggressively pursuing manufacturing/supply resiliency efforts. As appropriate, the Department will seek refinements to existing processes and develop new climate-specific plans and guidance.

Because of these current and ongoing concerns, the Department initiated in 2013 a review of existing directives, policies, manuals, and associated guidance documents and criteria to identify which ones should incorporate considerations of a changing climate. The initial screen reviewed 58 documents and identified 28 policies, programs and procedures for update; 5 have already been updated, all dealing with installations. During 2014, the Department will work within the existing review and update cycle to establish a plan for incorporating appropriate consideration of climate change into the relevant documents.

Many infrastructure managers are already adapting to changing climate factors. Reported rebuilding efforts after extreme storms include upgrading to more wind-resistant structures, burying utility lines underground, changing storage locations for chemicals used in low-lying wastewater treatment plants, protecting water supply wells, and removing vulnerable trees. In preparation for the possibility of more wildfires, installations reported preparing better firebreaks and making timber stand improvements to reduce fire fuel loads.

The Department has updated our master planning criteria for installations to require the consideration of climatic conditions, as well as mandating the consideration of changing climate conditions when designing buildings, including potential increased heating or cooling requirements. We also issued a Floodplain Management Policy in February 2014 that establishes requirements to minimize risks when military assets must be located within flood plains.

The Department is exploring the expansion of applications of risk management schemes already in use, primarily within the Defense Critical Infrastructure Program. Decisions on where and how to locate future infrastructure will become increasingly reliant on robust risk management processes that account for dynamic factors associated with the effects of climate change. While the initial modifications to risk management methodologies are focused on critical infrastructure, it is anticipated that the Department will utilize them across all decisionmaking in the future.

The Department has initiated several research and survey efforts to more fully identify and characterize vulnerabilities, impacts, and risks posed by climate change. The Department is implementing a phased installation-level vulnerability assessment approach to: develop methodologies for conducting consistent screening-level vulnerability assessments of military installations worldwide (starting with coastal and tidal installations); leverage recent scientific advancements regarding coastal assessment; and provide a platform to build upon prior to conducting more comprehensive and detailed assessments, whether coastal installations or otherwise.

A screening level survey assessment tool was piloted in the fall of 2013 and was deployed in 2014 to assess current installation-specific vulnerability to the impacts of climate-related events. Data from these screening-level assessments will be used to identify areas and installations where more detailed vulnerability assessments may be needed. The Department is using a whole-of government approach to develop recommendations on regional sea-level rise for use in more detailed coastal vulnerability and impact assessments of military installations worldwide, to ensure consistency in conducting these assessments.

As climate science advances, the Department will regularly reevaluate climate change risks and opportunities in order to develop policies and plans to manage its effects on the Department's operating environment, missions, and facilities. Research organizations within the Department, including the Strategic Environmental Research and Development Program (SERDP), are planning and completing studies to characterize climate change impacts in specific regions of the world and develop and pilot vulnerability assessment and adaptation methodologies and strategies.

Research to develop coastal assessment methods is scheduled for completion during 2014. Work in other regions is still underway, including research designed to understand how increased temperature trends and changes in the fire regime in the interior of Alaska will impact the dynamics of thawing permafrost and the subsequent effects on hydrology, access to training lands, and infrastructure; and how changes in storm patterns and sea levels will impact the Department's Pacific Island installations, including their water supplies.

The Department is actively conducting research that will support further integration of climate change into our considerations. This includes projects that: assess potential changes in the intensity, duration, and frequency of extreme precipitation events, including changes in the timing and intensity of snowmelt and subsequent runoff events; include development of adaptive decision frameworks; and address understanding the characteristics of species that are either conservation reliant or adaptable to potential changes in climate and human activities.

LONGER TERM: PLANS AND OPERATIONS

The longer term impacts of climate change may alter, limit, or constrain the environments in which our military will be operating. For example, sea level rise may impact the execution of amphibious landings; changing temperatures and lengthened seasons could impact timing windows for operations; and increased frequency of extreme weather could impact assumptions about flight conditions that could affect intelligence, surveillance, and reconnaissance capabilities.

The impacts of climate change may aggravate existing or trigger new risks to U.S. interests. Maintaining stability within and among other nations is an important means of avoiding full-scale military conflicts. The impacts of climate change may cause instability in other countries by impairing access to food and water, damaging infrastructure, spreading disease, uprooting and displacing large numbers of people, compelling mass migration, increasing competition for natural resources, interrupting commercial activity, or restricting electricity availability.

As Secretary of Defense Chuck Hagel said at the 2013 Halifax International Security Forum, ''Climate change does not directly cause conflict, but it can significantly add to the challenges of global instability, hunger, poverty, and conflict. Food and water shortages, pandemic disease, disputes over refugees and resources, more severe natural disasters—all place additional burdens on economies, societies, and institutions around the world.''

These developments could undermine already fragile governments that are unable to respond effectively or challenge currently stable governments, as well as increasing competition and tension between countries vying for limited resources. These gaps in governance can create an avenue for extremist ideologies and the conditions that foster terrorism.

As a Department, we are working to better understand how the impacts of climate change will affect plans and operations in the U.S. and abroad. The Department's unique capability to provide logistical, material, and security assistance on a massive scale or in rapid fashion may be called upon with increasing frequency. We are looking to identify early warning indicators for those areas critical to DOD's mission set, as well as conduct systematic regional and localized impact assessments to identify trends and where our resources should be focused.

The Department will be monitoring these developments and deciding which situations will require intervention based on U.S. security interests—either preemptively through security cooperation and capacity-building, or through stability operations if conditions escalate. We are exploring ways for the combatant commands to include in their missions noncombat support to address serious climate change-related U.S. national security vulnerabilities and to include climate considerations in their theater campaign plans.

We are currently working to integrate the impacts of climate change into our longer term planning scenarios, which articulate a range of future challenges that U.S. military forces must be prepared to confront. These scenarios support deliberations by DOD senior leadership on strategy and planning, programming, budgeting, and execution (PPBE) matters, including force sizing, shaping, and capability development.

We also plan to more fully integrate the impacts of climate change into our humanitarian assistance/disaster relief and other exercise plans, and are working to enhance the capacity of partner militaries and civil response readiness groups to plan for, and respond to, natural disasters. As noted in the 2014 QDR, "Climate change also creates both a need and an opportunity for nations to work together, which the Department will seize through a range of initiatives."

We also hope to more systematically harness resources beyond the traditional combatant command structure. This included the National Guard, and its State Partnership Program, service engineering units such as the U.S. Army Corps of Engineers and Naval Facilities Command, and OSD-led programs such as the Defense Environmental International Cooperation Program and the Strategic Environmental Research and Development Program.

To the extent that we are engaged in the construction of military and civilian infrastructure for partner nations, we are working to include consideration of climate change impacts on all our projects, ranging from site selection to resiliency planning.

Here in the U.S., State and local governments responding to the effects of extreme weather may seek increased defense support to civil authorities. The heightened demand, particularly on the National Guard and Reserve Component, could impact their availability for other contingencies or operations. We are in the process of exploring these implications and finding the right balance to ensure that our domestic needs can be met.

The Arctic

The effects of climate change are particularly acute in the Arctic region. Profound changes are already occurring that are having, and will continue to have, significant and long-lasting consequences. Over the coming decades, the Arctic will remain a remote, isolated, and complex environment; but over time, diminishing sea ice will make the Arctic Ocean increasingly accessible and used by Arctic as well as non-Arctic nations. At the same time, land access—which depends on frozen ground in much of the Arctic—will diminish as permafrost thaws.

Although some recent media reporting overstates the nature of current human activity and potential for military conflict in the near term, the U.S. Government, including DOD, must account for and closely monitor the long-term dynamics in the Arctic. Regardless of the rate and scale of change, we must be ready to contribute to national efforts in pursuit of strategic objectives in the region.

In response to these changing dynamics, the Department released a DOD Arctic Strategy in November 2013. The DOD Strategy supports the overarching national approach to the Arctic, embodied in the National Strategy for the Arctic region (released in May 2013): advancing U.S. security interests, pursuing responsible Arctic region stewardship, and strengthening international cooperation.

In accordance with the National strategy, the DOD Strategy seeks to preserve an Arctic region that is free of conflict, in which nations act responsibly and cooperatively, and where economic and energy resources are developed in a sustainable manner. In order to do so, we will ensure security, support safety, promote defense cooperation, and prepare for a wide range of challenges and contingencies.

The DOD Strategy recognizes that the U.S. Government response to changes in the Arctic requires a whole-of-government approach. In terms of preserving security, the U.S. Coast Guard in particular faces distinct near-term challenges. DOD continues to seek opportunities to coordinate our responses with the Coast Guard to leverage existing resources and avoid duplication of effort. We also continue to prepare ourselves to provide defense support for civil authorities when directed.

Our Arctic strategy will enable us to take a balanced approach to improving human and environmental security. Our challenge is to balance the risk of having inadequate capabilities or insufficient capacity appropriate for this changing region with the opportunity cost of making premature and/or unnecessary investments. We assess that the Arctic is a relatively low threat environment, and that existing DOD infrastructure and capabilities in the region are adequate to meet current U.S. defense needs in the near and midterm future.

Capabilities and requirements will need to reevaluated as conditions and regional activity change, and any gaps will need to be addressed. Given the low potential for armed conflict in the region, a buildup beyond what is required for existing DOD missions could send the wrong signal about our intentions for the region. We will continue to train and operate routinely in the region as we monitor the changing environment, revisit threat assessments, and take appropriate action as conditions change.

Given the nature of the Arctic, our approach to the region requires more than just interagency cooperation, it requires international cooperation. As we highlight in the 2014 QDR, relationships with allies and partners are important enablers for meeting our security and defense commitments. Our strategic approach to the Arctic reflects the relatively low level of military threat in a region bounded by nations that have not only publically committed to working within a common framework of international law and diplomatic engagement, but have also demonstrated the ability and commitment to do so.

We engage in frequent consultations with our Arctic partners, including through the Arctic Council, Northern Chiefs of Defense conference, the Arctic Security Forces Roundtable, and in Service-to-Service dialogues and exercises. Russia, one of five coastal Arctic states, has historically played a collaborative role in these forums. Although our near-term cooperation with Russia has been impacted by Russia's ongoing intervention in Ukraine, we continue to work with other Arctic partners and remain committed to the long-term objectives, approaches, and capabilities outlined in the Arctic Strategy.

INTERAGENCY COLLABORATION ON CLIMATE CHANGE

Partnerships are needed to fully ensure the Department's mission is sustainable given the effects of climate change. The Department cannot effectively assess its vulnerabilities and implement adaptive responses at its installations if neighbors and stakeholders are not part of the process. The Department's decisions and those of neighboring communities are intrinsically interconnected. Aspects of our mission, such as Force deployment, may be affected by assets outside our control, such as transportation infrastructure.

Understanding the complexities and uncertainties of climate change require a whole-of-government approach as well. Therefore, the Department already participates in nationwide efforts such as the U.S. Global Change Research Program, including the National Climate Assessment. It also partners with individual agencies such as the National Oceanic and Atmospheric Administration on, for example, the development and operational implementation of a national Earth System Prediction Capability.

The Department is also represented on interagency climate change councils and working groups and will continue to participate in federal climate partnerships and other interagency processes. The Department, through the Air Force Weather Agency, contributes earth-space environmental data, receiving nearly 500,000 weather observations and satellite-derived wind profiles each day and sharing these data with the National Climatic Data Center and the Navy's Fleet Numerical Meteorological and Oceanographic Center.

Climate change is an inherently global problem, and will require us to work closely with our allies, partners, and other countries across the world. As such, the State Department is leading our efforts to engage with the international community on these issues in multilateral forums and in bilateral relations. DOD is collaborating with and supporting the State Department in many of these initiatives, and we are continuing to develop new mechanisms and avenues for cooperation.

CONCLUSION

The effects of the changing climate affect the full range of Department activities, including plans, operations, training, infrastructure, acquisition, and longer term investments. The direction, degree, and rates of the physical changes will differ by region, as will the effects to the Department's mission and operations. By taking a proactive, flexible approach to assessment, analysis, and adaptation, the Department can keep pace with the impacts of changing climate patterns, minimize effects on the Department, and continue to protect our national security interests.

Senator MARKEY. Thank you.

Our next witness is Mr. Amos Hochstein, Deputy Assistant Secretary of State for Energy Diplomacy at the Department of State. Welcome.

STATEMENT OF AMOS J. HOCHSTEIN, DEPUTY ASSISTANT SECRETARY OF STATE FOR ENERGY DIPLOMACY, U.S. DEPARTMENT OF STATE, WASHINGTON, DC

Mr. HOCHSTEIN. Thank you, Mr. Chairman, Senator Murphy, for inviting me here to talk. I will summarize my testimony and, with your permission, have it submitted for the record in the longer version.

Mr. Chairman, as you said, recent developments that have been splashed across the front pages of newspapers across the globe serve as the latest reminders of the interplay between energy security, foreign policy, and our own national security. The critical nature of the geopolitics of energy is easily on display when you look at the global oil supply disruptions today, which are at historic levels of over 3 million barrels per day. Due to reduced output in Libya, Sudan, and South Sudan caused by political instability, politically induced declines in Nigeria and Venezuela, and reductions in Iran's exports by over 50 percent due to effective United States sanctions, it is now more important than ever that the United States and the State Department's Bureau of Energy Resources work diligently to ensure that energy resources are used to drive economic growth, prosperity, stability, and cooperation, rather than conflict.

Today's hearing is timely. Competition for access to, and control of, energy sources and supply routes can indeed be a source of conflict and revenues from energy sales can fuel and provide funds that prolong conflict. Poor governance of natural resources can also contribute to conflict. As you mentioned, Mr. Chairman, in your opening remarks about corruption, Senator Lugar, former chairman of this committee, said in sponsoring his legislation, ''The resource curse affects the United States as well as producing countries. It exacerbates global poverty, which can be a seedbed for terrorism. It empowers autocrats and dictators, and it can crimp world petroleum supplies by breeding instability.''

It is important to look at the global context. We are in the middle of a global energy transformation. On the demand side, we are seeing a historic shift where already non-OECD economies are surpassing and overtaking the OECD in total demand today and into the foreseeable future. On the supply side, production and delivery of energy is also changing dramatically. Energy supply is no longer concentrated in a small number of OPEC countries. New producers are joining their ranks.

As you said, nowhere is this transformation more evident than here in the United States. The dramatic shift in the United States energy balance has significantly impacted our national energy markets, as vast quantities of imported energy once destined for the United States have become available to other economies in Europe and in Asia.

Ukraine and Europe's dependence on Russian gas is a clear example of the risk of relying on any one dominant suppliers. The situation is urgent for Ukraine. While Ukrainian production is sufficient to cover summer demand, without Russian gas Ukraine will not be able to meet its consumption needs when the winter heating season resumes if those supplies from Russia are not continued. The short-term impact of this cutoff has been relatively small in Europe because it is not in the gas-intensive heating season and because last winter was mild, leaving stocks unseasonably high.

Our European energy security efforts intensified after Russia cut off gas supplies to Ukraine and European customers in 2009, advocating energy diversification across the European Continent. We work hand in hand with the EU Commission as well as with energy envoys in Eastern and Central European countries, meeting often with the ''V–4 Plus'' states. Second is diversity of import routes. Europe must build interconnected pipeline systems that allow gas to flow freely throughout the continent, unlike today. Finally, European countries must pursue diversification of sources, away from a dependence on any single supplier.

We are supporting Europe with actions as well as words. It is unlikely the Southern corridor would have become a reality without State Department engagement. We strongly support the creation of the Greece-Bulgaria Interconnector, which will allow gas from the Southern corridor from Azerbaijan to supply Southeast Europe, rather than just enter Central and Western Europe via Italy.

We support the EU's regulatory efforts in what is referred to as the Third Energy Package, which promotes market-based rules and fair competition, reducing Russia's ability to use its monopoly status as a weapon against its neighbors.

The value of energy diversification does not stop in Eastern Europe. Most of the Caribbean island states are significantly reliant on a single source for energy and European finance and similarly suffer from corruption and an inadequate investment climate. I recently joined Vice President Biden in Columbia and the Dominican Republic as he announced a new Caribbean Energy Security Initiative.

Existing offshore hydrocarbon discoveries in Israel and Cyprus, as well as potential offshore discoveries in Lebanon and Egypt, are transforming countries. I spend a lot of my time in the region helping to facilitate discussions between Israel, Cyprus, Lebanon, Jordan, and Egypt as these discoveries continue to play a role in redefining previous geopolitical relationships. Energy cooperation has significantly warmed relations between Israel and Cyprus, a point that was underscored by President Anastasiades when I was in Nicosia with Vice President Biden in May.

In Egypt, over the past 2 years I have made—in Egypt, similarly we expect to see deals potentially announced with Israel in the coming months. Over the past 2 years, I have made 16 trips to

Jordan to help facilitate solutions to Jordan's energy crisis, which was a result of terrorist bombings of the natural gas pipelines through Israel and Jordan. These efforts recently culminated in a historic deal for regionally competitive prices signed between Houston-based Noble Energy, operating offshore Israel, and the Jordanian industrial complex, saving Jordan billions and helping to stabilize its future economy.

Competing exclusive economic zone claims by Israel and Lebanon present a potential flashpoint for conflict as Lebanon continues to move forward with its first offshore exploration bid.

Closer to home, the State Department has brought negotiation to a successful completion and saw the U.S.-Mexico Transboundary Hydrocarbons Agreement enter into force with the support of the U.S. Senate.

Mr. Chairman, in conclusion, the energy diplomacy I have discussed today does not include all of our engagements around the world. The role of the State Department and the Energy Bureau in engaging these key energy security issues is now an integral part of our overall foreign policy and diplomacy. With wise stewardship of resources and by fostering private innovation and investment to expand energy access, we can ensure that the world's energy resources develop into a sustained driver of growth and stability, as opposed to conflict.

Thank you and I look forward to your questions.

[The prepared statement of Mr. Hochstein follows:]

PREPARED STATEMENT OF AMOS J. HOCHSTEIN

Thank you Chairman Markey, Senator Barrasso, and members of the subcommittee. I appreciate the opportunity to be here today to discuss energy security and conflict and how we are using our foreign policy tools to strengthen U.S. national security and global energy security. It is a privilege to be joined by my colleagues from the Department of Defense and the United States Agency for International Development (USAID).

Recent developments splashed across the front pages of newspapers around the globe serve as the latest reminders of the interplay between energy security and foreign policy. The critical nature of the geopolitics of energy is easily on display when you look at global oil supply disruptions, which are at historic levels of over 3 million barrels per day due to reduced output in Libya, Sudan and South Sudan caused by political instability, politically motivated declines in Nigeria and Venezuela, and reductions in Iran's exports by over 50 percent due to effective U.S. sanctions. It is now more important than ever that the United States and the State Department's Bureau of Energy Resources work diligently to ensure that energy resources are used to drive economic growth, stability, and cooperation, rather than conflict.

Today's hearing is timely. Competition for access to and control of energy sources and supply routes can indeed be a source of conflict, and revenues from energy sales can provide funds that prolong conflict. Poor governance of natural resources can also contribute to conflict by allowing pervasive corruption to undermine accountability, deprive economic growth, and encourage civil unrest. As your former colleague Senator Lugar said in sponsoring his legislation, "the 'resource curse' affects [the United States] as well as producing countries. It exacerbates global poverty, which can be a seedbed for terrorism, it empowers autocrats and dictators, and it can crimp world petroleum supplies by breeding instability."

We are in the middle of a global energy transformation that is affecting both supply and demand at the very same time. On the demand side, we are seeing a historic shift where already non-OECD economies have overtaken the OECD economies in total energy consumption. On the supply side, production and delivery of energy is also changing dramatically. Energy supply is no longer concentrated in a small number of OPEC countries—new producers are joining the ranks of major energy suppliers. We are seeing traditional and unconventional sources growing. We are seeing the growth of renewable energy. We are witnessing regional linkages, regional power lines, and the growing ability to move natural gas by ship, making energy markets increasingly global and competitive.

Nowhere is this transformation more evident than in the United States. The United States has increased oil production by 1 million barrels per day (bpd) in each of the last 2 years, and we are on track to replicate that this year. At the same time, the phase-in of increasingly robust efficiency efforts, such as Corporate Average Fuel Efficiency standards in the transportation sector, has reduced our oil demand, and helped slash net imports' share of U.S. oil consumption from 60 percent in 2005 to just over 30 percent today. Similarly, the United States has increased natural gas production by over 20 percent since 2007 because of growth from shale basins. This overall sea change in U.S. energy balances has had significant international energy market implications as vast quantities of imported energy once destined for the United States are now consumed elsewhere in the world markets.

TODAY'S UKRAINE CRISIS AND THE ENERGY CRISIS OF 2009

Ukraine and Europe's dependence on Russian gas is a clear example of the danger of relying on a dominant supplier.

After weeks of negotiations, Russia unfortunately ceased supplying gas to Ukraine on June 16, showing little willingness to continue negotiations until Ukraine pays its debt. The situation is urgent for Ukraine. While Ukrainian production is sufficient to cover summer demand, without Russian gas Ukraine will not be able to meet its consumption needs when the heating season resumes. The short-term impact of this cutoff has been relatively small in Europe because it is not in the gas-intensive heating season and because last year's winter was mild, leaving stocks unseasonably high. However, while there is no crisis in Europe today, it may be just around the corner. On an annual basis, Russia supplies more than half the gas consumed in Ukraine and more than a quarter of the gas consumed in the EU.

So where does that leave us today? While the media and others have focused on European energy security only for the last several months, the United States Government has been focused on this issue for several years.

Our European energy security efforts intensified after Russia cut off gas supplies to Ukraine and European customers in 2009. Since then, the State Department, now spearheaded by the Bureau of Energy Resources, has been intensely focused on energy security in Europe, advocating energy diversification across the European continent, particularly in Central and Eastern Europe. We work hand in hand with the EU Commission as well as with the Energy Envoys in Eastern/Central European countries meeting often with the ''V4 plus'' states.

When we talk about supply diversification in a European context, there are several components that must be addressed. First is fuel mix—including other energy sources like renewables and nuclear, as well as pursuing additional production from conventional and unconventional sources, potentially including shale basins.

Second is diversity of import routes. Europe must build an interconnected pipeline system that allows gas to flow freely throughout the continent. Finally, European countries must pursue diversification of sources away from a dependence on a single supplier. I am not suggesting that countries should eliminate Russian imports—that is neither necessary nor reasonable and Russia will remain a central player in the region—but introduction of alternative supplies will promote competition in the energy market. This will ultimately increase energy security while also benefiting consumers.

The United States is supporting Europe in actions as well as words. It is unlikely the Southern corridor would become a reality without State Department engagement. We strongly support the creation of the Greece-Bulgaria Interconnector, which will allow gas from the Southern corridor to supply Southeast Europe rather than just enter Central and Western Europe via Italy. For the same reason we support proposals to build an extension of the Southern corridor from Albania all the way to Croatia, once enough gas becomes available, ultimately supplying neighbors Hungary, Ukraine, and others.

We are working closely with colleagues in the EU Commission to advance interconnections of infrastructure in Central and Eastern Europe. These efforts are already producing successful projects such as the recent announcement of the Hungary-Slovakia interconnector. We also support proposals to build LNG terminals at critical points on European coasts, from Poland to Croatia to the Baltics. In short, Mr. Chairman, we agree with our European allies on the critical need for Europe to improve its energy infrastructure by constructing new pipelines, upgrading interconnectors to allow bidirectional flow, and building new LNG terminals to diversify fuel sources.

We support the EU's regulatory effort in what is referred to as the Third Energy Package, which has reduced Russia's ability to use its monopoly as a weapon against its neighbors. But more must be done to enforce these rules and their intent.

Part of the answer for Ukraine's energy security is its integration into the EU's energy market. However, before this integration can happen successfully, it is essential that Ukraine reform its energy sector. If it does not, and if corruption and inefficiency continue along with crippling energy subsidies for consumers, Ukraine will be right back where it started before long.

That is why the Bureau of Energy Resources and others in the U.S. Government are working with Ukraine on internal reform, governance, and efficiency improvements, as well as increasing their own gas production including by exploring their shale resource potential.

We have worked closely with the Governments of Ukraine, Hungary, Poland, and Slovakia and with European energy companies to see gas flowing from Europe into Ukraine. Thanks in part to these efforts, gas is now flowing from both Poland and Hungary into Ukraine. In late April, the Governments of Ukraine and Slovakia also signed an MOU on reverse-flow—an agreement which will allow gas to begin to flow from Slovakia into Ukraine as soon as September. Although the volumes will be small initially, they could increase significantly over the next year.

CARIBBEAN ENERGY SECURITY

The value of energy diversification does not stop in Eastern Europe. Most of the Caribbean island states are significantly reliant on a single source for energy and energy finance. Additionally, several suffer from inefficiency and aging infrastructure, corruption, and an investment climate that deters rather than encourages investment. As this is critical not only for the region as a whole, but also for our own national security, I recently joined Vice President Biden in Colombia and the Dominican Republic as he announced a new Caribbean Energy Security Initiative. The initiative will seek to address the barriers specific to this region and take actions to encourage the private sector to make the necessary investments.

No country in the world should rely on a single supplier whether in Europe, the Western Hemisphere, or Asia.

MEDITERRANEAN ENERGY AS AN ANCHOR FOR REGIONAL COOPERATION

The Eastern Mediterranean is an example of where, with active U.S. engagement, energy can serve as a catalyst to increase regional cooperation and avoid conflict.

Exciting offshore hydrocarbon discoveries in Israel and Cyprus, as well as potential offshore discoveries in Lebanon and Egypt, are transforming countries that were previously energy importers into countries that have the ability to both supply domestic demand, and export to regional and global markets where demand is high.

I have spent a lot of my time in the region helping to facilitate discussions between Israel, Cyprus, Lebanon, Jordan, and Egypt as these discoveries continue to play a pivotal role in redefining previous geopolitical relationships. Energy cooperation has significantly warmed relations between Israel and Cyprus—a point that was underscored by President Anastasiades when I was in Nicosia with Vice President Biden in May. Energy can also serve as an incentive to reaching a comprehensive settlement to the Cyprus question.

Also, repeated terrorist bombings of the Egyptian gas pipeline to Israel and Jordan forced Jordan to import expensive fuel oil to meet its energy needs—costing Jordan nearly $4 billion each year. Over the past 2 years I made 16 trips to Jordan to help facilitate solutions to Jordan's energy crisis. These efforts recently culminated in a historic deal signed between Houston-based Noble Energy operating offshore Israel, and a Jordanian industrial complex at regionally competitive prices, saving Jordan billions and helping to stabilize Jordan's future economy.

While the export of energy resources from Israel and Cyprus has the potential to forge stronger economic, and by extension diplomatic, ties, if managed poorly these resources could become the flash point for conflict.

Competing exclusive economic zone claims by Israel and Lebanon present a potential flash point for conflict if left unresolved. However, the United States continues to work closely with Israel and Lebanon to find a solution that will allow both countries to explore and exploit their offshore resources. We remain optimistic that a solution is possible because it is in the interest of both sides.

If countries in the region work together, the Eastern Mediterranean can become an important energy hub, promoting regional prosperity and supporting Europe's energy security. The United States will continue to support this effort.

Closer to home, the State Department was able to lead, with the Department of the Interior, an important international negotiation to defuse neighborly concerns over potential cross-boundary oil reserves in the Gulf of Mexico. We were able to see the negotiation to its successful completion and bring the United States-Mexico Transboundary Hydrocarbons Agreement into force with the support of the Congress.

Thanks to the increased certainty that this agreement brings, the United States was able to lease additional offshore Gulf of Mexico exploration blocks this year, earning the taxpayer some $21 million in bid payments that would not have accrued without this energy diplomacy.

CONCLUSION

Mr. Chairman, the energy diplomacy I have discussed today does not include all of ENR's global engagement. ENR's diplomacy spans the globe and extends from addressing oil and gas related-issues to advancing renewables and energy efficiency. With global oil supply outages at historic highs, patterns of energy production, consumption and trade fundamentally altered, and the sound energy supply footing of the United States, we have a historic opportunity to engage across the energy spectrum to address the many challenges that lie ahead. The role of the State Department and the Bureau of Energy Resources in engaging on these key energy security issues is now an integral part of our overall diplomacy. We have learned that in an interconnected world, we advance our own energy security and prosperity when our friends and allies advance with us. With the wise stewardship of resources, and by fostering private innovation and investment to expand energy access, we can ensure that the world's energy resources become a sustained driver of growth and stability, and not conflict.

Senator MARKEY. We thank you, Mr. Hochstein.

Finally, we are going to hear from Mr. Eric Postel, who is the Assistant Administrator for the Bureau of Economic Growth, Education and Environment for USAID. Welcome, Mr. Postel.

STATEMENT OF ERIC G. POSTEL, ASSISTANT ADMINISTRATOR FOR THE BUREAU OF ECONOMIC GROWTH, EDUCATION AND ENVIRONMENT, U.S. AGENCY FOR INTERNATIONAL DEVELOPMENT, WASHINGTON, DC

Mr. POSTEL. Thank you. On behalf of USAID, I would like to thank you, Chairman Markey, Ranking Member Barrasso, and Senator Murphy, for holding today's hearing and giving me the opportunity to testify. I request that my full statement be submitted for the record.

Senator MARKEY. Without objection.

Mr. POSTEL. Today I will highlight how a lack of clean energy access and/or an inability to address climate change risk can have a destabilizing effect on a country's economy, security, and the well-being of its citizens. Stability and well-being overseas often directly helps ensure U.S. national security. Today about 1.6 billion people, most of them living in developing countries, lack access to a reliable source of electricity. As a result, President Obama launched the Power Africa Initiative to promote a private sector solution to this shortage.

Expanding reliable energy access requires getting regulatory structures right while protecting vulnerable populations. Distortionary policies like fossil fuel subsidies can reduce incentives for energy efficiency, hamper low or no-carbon energy production, raise dependence on energy imports, and create unsustainable fiscal liabilities. One striking example is a country that several have already mentioned today, which is the Ukraine, where the U.S. Government is now working with Ukrainians to bring electric rates to a level that covers costs, to protect the most vulnerable from the impact of gas and heating rate increases, to strengthen payment discipline, to improve energy efficiency in the heating sector, and to increase transparency.

For many countries, renewable energy such as solar or wind has begun to play an important role in meeting their energy needs. As the cost of renewable energy declines, many countries are scaling up renewables for a variety of reasons, including cost, domestic energy security, and addressing climate change. As a result, USAID is working to expand the use of renewables in countries such as India, Philippines, South Africa, and Ethiopia. In Ethiopia, Power Africa, for example, is helping develop Corbetti, a 1,000-megawatt geothermal plant that will be the largest geothermal plant in East Africa and the country's first privately owned energy project.

Improving a country's resilience to adverse climate change impacts is essential to economic growth, stability, and security. It also protects our development assistance investments. Floods, droughts, cyclones, and extreme temperature constitute 75 percent of natural disasters globally and affect more than 200 million people annually.

Focusing on building resilience also saves money. Disaster planning efforts are cheaper than relief efforts and reconstruction. The World Bank estimates that every dollar used for disaster risk reduction has a $7.00-savings in disaster recovery costs. So, for example, USAID and NASA are helping Bangladesh adopt a new flood forecasting system to reduce the losses associated with the large-scale flooding that occurs in that country most years.

In many of the world's poorest countries, agriculture plays a substantial role in their economies, but adverse climate impacts can reduce agricultural productivity and output and in extreme cases cause widespread food insecurity.

USAID has begun working to make our agriculture investments more resilient to weather variability. In Ethiopia we are working to increase agricultural incomes and enhance resilience to climate change for up to 15 million people. In Senegal and the Dominican Republic, we are working with the local insurance companies to help them build the expertise to design and market affordable weather-based insurance that can reach small rural households whose livelihoods depend on that weather.

Improving and sustaining access to water in the face of more frequent and severe droughts is another important element of our approach. Our programs in the Sahel work to increase access to water by repairing and improving water access points, building appropriate irrigation infrastructure, and introducing practices to improve water conservation and filtration.

USAID is also working to reduce greenhouse gas emissions by addressing deforestation and land use change.

For example, we are working with the Tropical Forest Alliance 2020, a public-private partnership of more than 400 companies, to reduce deforestation associated with key global commodities.

In conclusion, we see a clear set of linkages between our efforts to improve energy access and address the impacts of climate change with our national security. Thank you for the opportunity to testify this afternoon and I look forward to your questions.

[The prepared statement of Mr. Postel follows:]

PREPARED STATEMENT OF ERIC G. POSTEL

Chairman Markey, Ranking Member Barrasso, and members of the subcommittee, on behalf of the U.S. Agency for International Development (USAID), I would like to thank you for holding today's hearing and giving me the opportunity to testify.

President Obama set forth a new vision of a results-driven USAID that would lead the world in development. We have risen to this challenge, pioneering a new model of development that emphasizes partnerships, innovation, and results. We are guided in these efforts by our new mission statement: we partner to end extreme poverty and promote resilient democratic societies while advancing our security and prosperity.

In today's global economy, America's well-being and economic growth are closely linked to economic growth in the developing world. Growth in developing countries helps to create new and better markets for U.S. goods and services. Equally important, stable, secure, and resilient nations are less vulnerable to crises, illegal activity, and international crime, which directly impacts U.S. national security.

Two factors that are critical to spurring and maintaining economic growth and stability in developing countries are access to affordable, clean energy and the existence of social and institutional capacity to adapt to, mitigate and recover from shocks and stresses such as economic downturns and the adverse impacts of climate change. In particular, working with developing countries to help them deal with destabilizing climate change consequences, including water supply shortages, coastal flooding and droughts, is critical. Such work also protects our current and future development investments.

Today, I will highlight how the lack of clean energy access and the inability to address climate change risks can have a destabilizing effect on a country's economy, security, and the well-being of its citizens. I will describe USAID's efforts to address these challenges and discuss how our work on adaptation to climate change, water security, food security, and sustainable landscapes impacts security. Much of this work is embodied in USAID's Climate Change and Development Strategy, which seeks to help developing countries speed their transition to climate resilient, low emission, sustainable economic growth. Stability and well-being overseas often directly helps ensure U.S. national security.

ENERGY ACCESS

Today, about 1.6 billion people, most of them living in the developing world, lack access to a reliable source of electricity. The economic consequences of this are enormous. The availability and reliability of affordable energy—especially electricity— is critical to growing businesses, both large and small, creating jobs, developing markets, and providing a range of social services such as health care, education and public security.

This was clearly seen when the U.S. Government assessed constraints to economic growth in Africa 2 years ago. As a result, the administration launched the Power Africa initiative to promote a private-sector solution to improved electricity services. This initiative has made considerable progress already, with nearly 2,800 megawatts (MW) of new generation projects financially closed, and another 5,000 MW in the planning stages.

Expanding reliable energy access requires getting regulatory structures right while protecting vulnerable populations. Distortionary policies like fossil fuel subsidies can reduce incentives for energy efficiency, hamper low and no carbon energy production, raise dependence on energy imports, and create unsustainable fiscal liabilities. One striking example is in Ukraine, where the U.S. Government is now working with Ukrainian Government to bring electric rates to a level that covers costs, protect the most vulnerable from the impact of gas and heating rate increases, strengthen payment discipline, improve energy efficiency in the heating sector, and increase transparency.

For many countries, renewable energy, such as solar, wind and hydropower, has begun to play an important role in meeting emerging energy needs. USAID is supporting these efforts through our development programs. Around the world, the cost of renewables is becoming competitive with hydrocarbon-based power generation, while also helping to mitigate the destabilizing effects of high-priced hydrocarbons. As the cost of renewable energy declines, many countries are scaling up renewables for a variety of reasons, including cost, domestic energy security and addressing climate change. We will work with the Department of State and other agencies to ensure relevant U.S. renewable energy solutions contribute to these developments.

With USAID support a number of countries are scaling up renewables. For example, India is scaling up wind and solar energy generation. USAID's partnership with India in this area is focused on energy sector reform, energy access, and clean energy programming, and has helped India develop 30,000 MW of wind, solar and small hydro generation capacity with a goal of adding another 30,000 MW between 2012 and 2017. This will be almost 25 percent of India's total generation capacity in 2017. Renewables not only help India to increase power generation and weather the shock of volatile hydrocarbon prices, but also help reduce the country's greenhouse gas emissions.

South Africa is another example where affordable electricity plays a critical role in supporting economic growth and stability. South Africa has recently begun to scale up wind and solar generation through private investment. Between 2011 and 2013, South Africa's national power company, Eskom, signed purchase agreements for almost 3,600 MW of renewable energy generation. South Africa is addressing its electricity crisis by diversifying its energy mix, and USAID is supporting several programs that will help South Africa in this important effort with a new program that focuses on renewable energy development.

In Ethiopia, Power Africa is helping develop Corbetti, a 1,000 MW geothermal plant in Ethiopia's Rift Valley. When complete, Corbetti will be the largest geothermal project in East Africa and the first privately owned energy project in Ethiopia, paving the way for other private sector investors looking at Ethiopia for opportunities. Corbetti and the development of Ethiopia's rich geothermal resources will help the country diversify beyond hydro.

In the Philippines, USAID has been working successfully on scaling up renewable energy and energy sector reform. These two areas are closely interrelated as reformed energy systems are more capable of providing the funds and people needed to increase modern energy access and scale-up clean energy. USAID supported the Philippines by helping them to pass a biofuels law that allowed them to utilize coconut oils as a mix to their fuel supplies. More recently, USAID helped the government to put into place a National Renewable Energy Plan and establish feed in tariffs that are designed to be sustainable, which will help the government to achieve a significant scaling up of renewable energy in the coming decades.

For the Philippines, the development of renewable energy sources is increasingly important given the rising tensions in areas through which fuel supplies must flow. The southern island of Mindanao, one of the Philippines' fastest growing regions, historically plagued by insurgency and instability, is dependent on hydropower generated by a limited number of dams. Long-term climate forecasts suggest this region will experience decreased rainfall in the future if climate trends continue, thus reducing the availability of water to power the dams. Risks to hydropower supplies are a crucial energy security issue for the region. Diversification of energy supplies is therefore essential for prosperity in the region and USAID is working to help increase the role of renewables in the island's overall power supply.

Scaling up renewable energy in countries like the India, Philippines, and South Africa serves multiple objectives, supporting economic growth, and serving the U.S. interest in stability and sustainable growth, and mitigating the risks of climate change.

CLIMATE CHANGE

Improving a country's resilience to adverse climate change impacts is essential to its economic growth, stability, and security. It also protects our development assistance investments. Focusing on building resilience also saves money: disaster planning efforts that reduce storm damages are cheaper than relief efforts and infrastructure reconstruction. The World Bank estimates indicate that every dollar used for disaster risk reduction has a seven dollar savings in disaster recovery costs.

I would like to discuss some of the destabilizing effects climate change can have in terms of creating national disasters, reducing agricultural productivity and causing food insecurity, and depleting water supplies and how USAID is addressing them, particularly through USAID's Climate Change and Development Strategy.

Floods, droughts, cyclones and extreme temperatures constitute 75 percent of natural disasters globally and affect more than 200 million people annually. These types of disasters are expected to intensify with climate change.

In Bangladesh, more than 20 percent of the country is flooded in a normal year, leading to lives lost and the destruction property. Shifting monsoon patterns are expected to increase discharge of the rivers into Bangladesh, worsening flooding; this will be particularly problematic in combination with sea level rise. To improve the country's ability to mitigate the impact of flooding, USAID and NASA, through a joint effort called SERVIR, are helping Bangladesh adopt a new flood forecasting system. Under SERVIR, data gathered is enabling Bangladesh to provide an additional 5 days of warning about impending floods. Before this program, flood warnings were issued 3 days in advance, which does not provide adequate time for farmers and their families to prepare. USAID is also working with the U.S. Army Corps of Engineers to ensure that storm shelters are built well and appropriately to reduce loss of life.

In the Philippines, USAID worked to restore water services in the wake of Typhoon Haiyan and is now supporting local water utilities and the national government in undertaking long-term planning that can help to ensure reliable water supplies in the context of increasing climate stress. We are also working in partnership with local Philippine institutions on the sustainability of these projects.

In many of the world's poorest countries agriculture plays a substantial role in the nation's economy and employs a large portion of its workforce. Adverse climate impacts such as erratic weather patterns, drought, and flooding can reduce agricultural productivity and output, severely challenging traditional agricultural livelihoods and in extreme cases causing widespread food insecurity and contributing to famine, as seen in the large scale humanitarian emergencies in the Horn of Africa and Sahel in 2011 and 2012. Improving local-level resilience to the impacts of climate change can protect and enhance agricultural production for local, regional and global benefit, and mitigate the disruptive influence of climate-related shocks.

USAID has begun working to make our food security investments more resilient to the impacts of current weather variability and longer term changes in climate. In Ethiopia, USAID is supporting an effort to increase household incomes and enhance resilience to climate change in the country's southern and eastern pastoralist regions, home to about 15 million people. The pastoralist population chiefly raises livestock in arid lowlands, which are susceptible to frequent, and often severe, droughts that put millions of people at increased risk of food scarcity. The range of activities supported includes: increasing climate change awareness and early warning of droughts, mapping rangelands, rehabilitating damaged grazing grounds, building water storage, improving animal health and nutrition, and increasing pastoralist access to finance. Programs help develop innovative approaches that link scientific and local knowledge by tailoring information to the needs of both pastoralist communities and government stakeholders to improve decision making and reduce risk.

USAID also supports partners that are developing and testing weather-index insurance. Index insurance is a tool that can help populations whose livelihoods depend on the weather—such as small farmers and pastoralist herders—to manage changing climate risks. In Ethiopia, Senegal, and the Dominican Republic, USAID is working with local insurance companies to help them build the expertise to design and market affordable, weather-based insurance that can reach rural households.

Climate change also impacts water availability, quality and access. Where there is weak institutional capacity to constructively adapt to changes in water variability or to respond to extreme events like droughts, conflict risks are heightened.

Improving and sustaining access to water in the face of more frequent and severe droughts is an important element of USAID's approach to building resilience in areas affected by fragility like the Sahel, where many depend on rain-fed agriculture and pasture for their livelihoods. USAID's programs in the Sahel work to increase access to water through repairing and improving water access points, building appropriate irrigation infrastructure, and introducing practices to improve water conservation and filtration. Our programs help communities to better manage their natural resources and reduce the potential for conflict over water and other scarce resources. These investments are intended to increase the ability of people, communities, and countries to better cope with shocks and stresses including climate variability and change, and ultimately, reduces the need for humanitarian interventions.

Another aspect of USAID's climate change efforts—promoting sustainable landscapes—also addresses drivers of instability and food insecurity. Deforestation and degradation of forests, coastal wetlands and other landscapes, not only increase greenhouse gas emissions, but also deplete natural resource assets over the long term and hurt economic activities that depend on healthy ecosystems. Deforestation can also be a destabilizing force in many forest-dependent communities, and illegal deforestation has been associated with corruption or criminal activity in a range of countries.

USAID is working to reduce greenhouse gas emissions by addressing the drivers of deforestation and land-use change: unsustainable forest clearing for agriculture, illegal logging, poor governance of land and forests, and a failure to ensure that local communities benefit economically from sustainable forest and land management. For example, in Colombia, USAID is working to improve the national government's management of biodiversity-rich forests, helping to ensure that Colombia's natural resources will not be used for illicit purposes. Another example of USAID's work in this area is the Tropical Forest Alliance 2020, a public-private partnership with a network of more than 400 companies. The Tropical Forest Alliance's goal is to reduce tropical deforestation associated with key global commodities, such as palm oil, soy, beef, and paper and pulp. Also, the Coral Triangle Initiative with USAID support is working to conserve imperiled coral reef ecosystems.

CONCLUDING REMARKS

We see a clear set of linkages between USAID's efforts to improve energy access and address the impacts of climate change and regional security, which in turn benefits our national security. Heavy dependence on imported energy is often a major economic challenge due to fluctuating prices and pressures on foreign exchange reserves. Many countries—especially those with limited domestic hydrocarbon resources—are finding that scaling up renewables is a viable option, particularly as the costs of wind and solar decline. And reducing reliance of vulnerable economies to energy supplies from volatile regions has multiple development, diplomatic and security benefits for the United States.

USAID's work in our climate programs is about smarter development—investments that avoid future costs and crises, use modern technology and innovations to leapfrog development stages, and leverage local actors and the private sector to help scale our investments and ensure sustainability. Preventing or mitigating tomorrow's disasters—whether famine, drought, water shortages, or damage from severe weather events—enhances regional security, reduces hits to economic growth, and benefits the United States.

Senator MARKEY. Thank you, Mr. Postel.

The chair will recognize himself. Let me ask you this, Dr. Chiu. Does the Defense Department take a wait and see attitude on climate change and the risks that it poses, or does it integrate climate change into its future planning in terms of our ability to be able to properly anticipate the challenges to our country?

Dr. CHIU. I believe the answer is the latter. We are integrating it into our future planning. Let me give you an example of how we are thinking about that. We have a lot of experience doing humanitarian assistance and disaster relief operations. Commander PACCOM, for example, speaks a lot about the demands that he has for providing that kind of assistance to our allies and partners in the Asia-Pacific region. Currently our ability to plan for these has been—or in the past our ability to plan for these has largely been an extrapolation of past efforts, and we have literally looked backward, for example, at the last 10 years and kind of projected the same incidents and severity going forward to plan for our activities.

We have increasingly found that that is not an appropriate methodology for looking at future challenges. We are now taking into account the variability provided to us by the data that NOAA, the Navy's Oceanographer's Office and other scientific sources provide us for then looking at the potential for increased incidents of extreme weather and what that will do for the demand signal. So that is one example of how we are beginning to integrate into our future planning.

Senator MARKEY. Thank you.

Mr. Postel, a lot of people say that energy is just another commodity and we should just treat it that way; it is no different than anything else; it is like a watch or a computer chip. But when I look at USAID I see a lot of focus on food, on agriculture, on energy. Can you talk a little bit about how important it is for a country to have their own energy capacity so that they are not dependent upon other countries?

Mr. POSTEL. Thank you for your question, Senator, and thank you for your support of a number of USAID's activities.

The thing is about energy is that it is used across all sectors. So even if we are talking about a health clinic in Haiti where the lights go out because there is insufficient energy supply, putting the doctors in a real difficult situation in terms of the patients who may be on the operating table, to agriculture, where you need energy in a variety of aspects of that, across all sectors of economies and human endeavor, you need energy. How do we study in classrooms if we do not have energy in a lot of aspects of that?

So we feel that the energy requirement is needed as it affects all aspects of development. Then you start to get into the issue of energy diversification and not necessarily relying on just one source, as one of the witnesses talked about, and lastly in terms of affordability, that when countries are able to diversify away from strictly imported sources of energy we see a lot of advantages of that economically for the country.

Senator MARKEY. Thank you.

Mr. Hochstein, do you agree with that? Do you agree that energy plays such a significant role that it has to be treated differently than any other commodity in the world?

Mr. HOCHSTEIN. I think I would. Energy is—I think there are a lot of commodities—there are a number of commodities that probably would fit into categories where we would want to take particular care, but energy clearly has an impact across the broader economy, as Eric Postel just said. Without reliable, affordable access to electricity and energy resources, it is difficult to see economies grow and develop and lower businesses develop into mid-sized businesses and so on, without that kind of access to affordable and reliable energy.

Senator MARKEY. The bottom line is that we fight trade wars over automobiles or over computer chips. We fight real wars over food and energy. That is just the bottom line and what differentiates those commodities. We just have to keep that always in the front of our mind.

Mr. Hochstein, do you agree that there is a real problem that is taking place with ISIS in terms of the supply of oil to the global market potentially in Iraq and across that region?

Mr. HOCHSTEIN. Let me limit my comments to what we can say in this forum, sir. Clearly, we are very troubled by everything about ISIS, including the fact that they have been able to secure energy resources and energy fields, refineries, on both sides of the Syria-Iraq border. I think it is very troubling.

Senator MARKEY. Well, there have been news reports that ISIS is raising about $1 million per day selling Iraqi and Syrian oil on the black market. Can you confirm those figures?

Mr. HOCHSTEIN. I have seen those stories and probably in this hearing, in this session, I probably cannot go into greater detail. But I think there is no doubt that they are in control of some of the energy resources in Iraq.

Senator MARKEY. Iraqi oil production recently rose to 3 million barrels per day, a level higher actually than the pre-United States invasion levels, making it the eighth-largest oil producer in the world. Most of the oil is exported. For the moment, ISIS has not pushed into southern Iraq, where the majority of the country's oil is produced. If they did, even if they threatened to, there could be a major impact in production from southern Iraq, some have estimated potentially a loss of upward of 1.5 million barrels per day. That could raise prices dramatically all across the planet. Can you talk a little bit about that?

Mr. HOCHSTEIN. Yes. As you said, Mr. Chairman, Iraq's oil production is largely in two places. One is in the south in the Basra region, which is the southern tip of Iraq on the Persian or the Arabian Gulf. Its production has risen consistently over the last few years, to some degree against the odds, and its exports stand today at about 2.6, 2.7 million barrels a day. So they are a tremendous contributor to global oil supplies and to stability in the oil markets.

Especially, the substantial rise in oil supplies out of Iraq came at the same time that we were restricting a lot of oil supplies out of Iran. So it very much supplied that kind of balance.

The other area where it is an emerging area for oil production is in the north, in the Kurdistan region, the KRG. Both of those areas are still under the control of the Iraqi Government and the government of the KRG.

Senator MARKEY. Thank you.

Senator Barrasso.

Senator BARRASSO. Thank you, Mr. Chairman.

Secretary Chiu, today's hearing focuses on U.S. security implications of energy and climate policy. And I agree, there are serious implications for our national security, and you see them by the climate policies being implemented in places like Europe. Global international crime syndicates are manipulating these policies for profit. These groups use funds from manipulating these green policies to aid and support terrorist organizations and drug cartels that wish to do us and our allies harm.

Europol, the European Union's law enforcement agency that handles criminal intelligence, issued a threat assessment in June of 2013. Now, I have asked that this threat assessment be entered into the record, Mr. Chairman.

Senator MARKEY. Without objection.

[EDITOR'S NOTE.—The threat assessment article mentioned above was too voluminous to include in the printed hearing. It will be retained in the permanent record of the committee.]

Senator BARRASSO. The threat assessment states that, ''There are increasing reports of Italian organized crime groups engaging in a so-called alternative or green energy market.'' The threat assessment highlights a mafia in Italy which it calls one of the most threatening organized crime groups at the global level. They state in the report—they cite a study that says the crime group earns 44 billion euros a year in income from its illicit activities. The group has forged close alliances with Mexican and Colombian drug cartels, has gained a foothold in the United States and Canada, recently been implicated in money laundering, a well-known terrorist organization. The Europol threat assessment clearly states this group is, ''involved in environmental crime.''

I have similar assessments from Canada, from the Canadian Government, on money-laundering and terrorist activity financing watch; also from Interpol; and I would like those also entered into the record, Mr. Chairman.

Senator MARKEY. Without objection.

[EDITOR'S NOTE.—The Canadian Government assessment mentioned above was too voluminous to include in the printed hearing. It will be retained in the permanent record of the committee.]

Senator BARRASSO. So I ask you, Mr. Secretary: Are there serious unintended consequences to our national security if we go down this path, as Europe has done, in adopting such policies that can be so easily exploited to fund nonstate criminal or terrorist elements; folks that wish to do us harm?

Dr. CHIU. Senator, my interpretation of the facts that you have presented is that transnational crime, as we have seen in many different sectors, is attracted to where the money is, and we see that across many different types of sectors. Transnational crime as an element of concern for our national security, you are absolutely correct, is something that we have to pay attention to. But I believe it is the economic incentives for this, rather than climate change or the effects of climate change, which the Department is focused on, that are the causes of this.

Senator BARRASSO. So the solution offered of a similar scheme like that can run itself into significant problems from the standpoint of organized crime, with the solution that those countries have come up with.

Next, in October 2003 Peter Schwartz and Doug Randall released a report, "An Abrupt Climate Change Scenario and Its Implications for the United States National Security." This is a number of years ago, which was commissioned by Andrew Marshall, Director of the United States Department of Defense Office of Net Assessment. I ask, Mr. Chairman, this be put in the record as well.

Senator MARKEY. Without objection.

[EDITOR'S NOTE.—The report mentioned above was too voluminous to include in the printed hearing. It will be retained in the permanent record of the committee.]

Senator BARRASSO. It states that "Even the most sophisticated models cannot predict the details of how the climate change will unfold, which regions will be impacted in which ways, and how governments and societies might respond."

So I say, why should we then spend billions of taxpayer dollars, defense dollars specifically, on climate change predictions about future conflicts due to drought and famine that the Department's own studies say that we cannot predict? Is this not just wasteful spending based on faulty predictions, given all of our other defense needs to fight terrorism abroad?

Dr. CHIU. In totality, that particular report, which was done to look at a very long-term timeframe, decades-out timeframe, says it is difficult to predict, but we must consider the range of possibilities, which is exactly what we do in the Department of Defense. I am not aware of any billions of dollars of U.S. Department of Defense money that are being spent on predictions. In fact, what I am talking about here is mostly taking into consideration, like many other trends that we take into consideration, to ensure that we are prepared should these events occur.

In some of these cases, we are recommending, frankly, monitoring to additionally consider those trends. In some of these cases, there will be specific activities, particularly in the near term the installation pieces that I have already mentioned that we do have to manage and adapt to today.

Senator BARRASSO. But it is interesting, because the DOD-commissioned report, as you say, it is very difficult to make these clear predictions, and what do you protect and prevent against. It says in 2007 a particular severe storm could cause the ocean to break through levies in the Netherlands, making a few key coastal cities such as The Hague unlivable. The report also predicts that between 2010–2020 Europe, ''struggles to stem emigration out of Scandinavian and Northern European nations in search of warmth.''

So it would be interesting—there is a prediction that by 2018 Russia will join the European Union. So if we had spent our defense dollars based on these types of predictions—and you talked about using defense dollars to protect ourselves as we look at all of these potential predictions—we would have wasted billions of scarce defense dollars.

My point is, are we not just betting our scarce national security dollars on a risky bet by making predictions about weather, climate, years into the future a major national security priority?

Dr. CHIU. As I have said, Senator, we have not done that. We have not either made those predictions or invested in those scenarios. Moreover, sir, as you said yourself, the report points out that one cannot predict those events. I believe they were trying to represent kind of the range of possible severe events, which is what they did, but that is all that they did. It painted a range of possibilities that we needed to take into consideration. I think we have effectively, and I think you have seen our investments with regard to those.

Senator BARRASSO. In March of this year, Jeff Kueter, President of the George Marshall Institute, released a study called ''The Climate of Insecurity.'' Mr. Chairman, I ask that this be entered into the record.

Senator MARKEY. Without objection.

[EDITOR'S NOTE.—The study mentioned above can be found in the ''Material Submitted for the Record'' section of this hearing.]

Senator BARRASSO. Thank you, Mr. Chairman.

The report says: ''Efforts to link climate change to the deterioration of U.S. national security rely on improbable scenarios, imprecise and speculative methods, and scant empirical support.'' The report goes on to say—and this is just March of this year. It says: ''Accepting the connection can lead to the dangerous expansion of U.S. security concerns, inappropriately applied resources, and diversion of attention from more effective responses to known environmental problems.''

It also provides information to show that factors other than the environment were much more significant in explaining the onset of conflict. A recent survey cited in the report found that primary causes of interstate conflict and civil war are political, not environmental.

So do you disagree that the primary cause of conflict and war is political, not environmental?

Dr. CHIU. No, sir, I do not disagree with that. But I do believe that a lot of the politics can be driven by the effects of climate change, including, as we have mentioned today, things like water shortages, food shortages, extreme weather, mass migration as a result of these.

I would point out, I am not familiar with that very specific report, but the work that I am describing here is not so much thinking of climate change as in, and of itself, deteriorating U.S. national security, but really that the effects of climate change need to be taken into consideration as we seek to protect U.S. national security interests, along with the many other trends and drivers of these types of phenomena that you have suggested.

Senator BARRASSO. Because it is interesting, when you take a look at what the Secretary of State has talked about as kind of the greatest, the most—''the world's most fearsome weapon of mass destruction'' is what Secretary of State Kerry has called climate change. But you are agreeing that the primary cause of conflict and war is political, not environmental.

Thank you, Mr. Chairman.

Senator MARKEY. The Senator from Connecticut.

Senator MURPHY. Thank you very much, Mr. Chairman.

Thank you to the witnesses for being here today. Just a quick comment on the beginning of the line of questioning from Senator Barrasso. I think we all appreciate the caution about the ability of criminals to infiltrate renewable energy markets. As a representative of a State that has lost hundreds of millions of dollars in bad investments with Enron, one particular conventional energy company, we know that fraud is not limited to the renewable energy markets, and in fact, criminals have found their way into virtually every industry in which you could make some money and across the globe. That is an invitation to go after the criminals and the syndicates rather than to divest our interest and money from those particular industries.

Let me start with you, Mr. Hochstein, and talk a little bit about Ukraine and Russia again. We have had a heck of a time getting an energy efficiency bill, a fairly modest piece of legislation, through the United States Senate. It strikes me as an imperative for this country to get serious about using less energy, which is a win-win. We make ourselves less dependent on foreign sources and we save the government and private industry some money along the way.

But this is a big part of the story about why Ukraine has gotten in as much trouble as they have gotten into. Their dependency on Russia is due to the fact that they do not have domestic resources or alternative sources, but also because they waste an enormous amount of energy. If you sort of talk about what really is compromising Ukrainian national sovereignty today, you would put energy efficiency at the top of the list—these old Soviet distribution systems by which one giant boiler, set of boilers, is responsible for heating and transmitting heat to an entire neighborhood, in which the majority of that heat is lost along the way.

When you talk about national security for Ukraine right now, well, they want to look for shale oil and they want to be able to bring in new energy resources. When you talk to the Ukrainian leadership themselves, at the top of their list is energy efficiency, is that not right?

Mr. HOCHSTEIN. Yes, sir. I think, Senator, you articulated it quite right. I think that—there is a number of issues that we need to work with Ukraine and that we would like to help them with. But you are correct that before you can get to the point of looking at some of the financial issues there is two base points that have to be addressed. The first is protecting this industry and this sector from corruption, as has been the case for the last several decades, which has contributed to where they are today.

The inefficiency of the system, as you have just described, is right on the mark. The easiest dollar to save is the one that you do not spend. If you can get the systems to be far more efficient and to address the subsidies that, in a gradual way, that encourage inefficiency in the system, and if we can address all these fundamental issues in the sector, plus have the advantage of increasing production from unconventional sources, conventional sources, and looking at some of the other work, that would go a long way to solving their dependence on the single source on Russia.

To that end, we are working. Already we have identified areas that we will be giving some technical expertise. We are working as a whole-of-government approach on this. We work closely with our colleagues from USAID in some of the efforts on efficiency, on introduction of other sources of energy, like renewables, into the system. I am looking, working with the Department of Energy on the areas of technical advice to increase the amount of conventional gas that they can produce in the short term, short to medium term, and in the longer term looking at what we can do on the unconventional side.

Senator MURPHY. As we look to the ways in which countries would comply with a new global agreement on carbon emissions, efficiency is the quickest and easiest way to get there. So if we are looking at ways to try to provide some incentives for countries that are far behind the curve in terms of energy efficiency, which compromises their security, as is the case with Ukraine, a global carbon reduction agreement is going to be one of the fastest ways to try to prompt countries to get serious about energy efficiency.

Mr. HOCHSTEIN. I would presume that is correct. I would note that we have a special envoy on climate change and he works on a lot of those areas and I do not. But the baseline where we work together and we all come together is on the areas of efficiency. It clearly is something that we need to encourage more of because it will get us towards those goals that you described just now.

Senator MURPHY. I pose this question to Mr. Postel, but either of the other panel members can comment on this. Let us try to look ahead to what some of the next global scarcity crises are. You talked a little bit in your presentation about water scarcity. I think about India and Bangladesh, where you do a lot of work at the top of the list. These are countries, India in particular, which rely on the Tibetan Plateau in order to receive the majority of the natural water resources that they use. Reports are that in the northern portion of India the glaciers have retreated over the last three to five decades by 25 to 35 percent, that they may be gone by 2050.

This is a crisis waiting to happen, a country with simmering instability to begin with, a bursting population. I am talking about India is on the verge of potentially losing the major source of natural water, the Tibetan Plateau glaciers.

I know you are doing a lot of work on this issue, USAID is, something I am sure the Department of State worries about. Talk about the potential for water instability in a country like India should we not reverse the damage done to the biggest source of their water?

Mr. POSTEL. Thank you for your question, Senator, and thank you for your support of USAID's development work. As you just described, in that situation and some other situations if you have these big changes that affect water, which could occur for any number of reasons, but if you lose those glaciers, you could have a whole series of things initially. As all that snow starts and ice starts converting into water, you could actually have an abundance of water, and there are issues that have happened. Then afterward, of course, once it is gone it is gone, and then we have to look at things like water conservation and what are the other possibilities, because you could have many, many people without water.

So I do not want to speculate about—I am not familiar with specific modeling, but we see this in several different places around the world where there are these possibilities and we are trying to think through how can we respond in those circumstances, how can we be more efficient with water and so forth.

Senator MURPHY. One of the ways, as you know because again USAID has done an enormous amount of work on this—and if you allow me, Mr. Chairman, I will just make this one final comment— is around the issue of clean cook stoves. There are 3 billion people worldwide who do their cooking on rudimentary stoves using wood or some other form of biomass. That is a particular issue in India and much of that black carbon, which is a super pollutant, is essentially landing in the region that is heating up those glaciers.

Senator Collins and I have a piece of legislation that we have just introduced which would help to supplement the work that USAID and State and others have done on this initiative. But I applaud all of your work. This is a crisis happening and waiting to happen at an even greater level and this is a quick way to try to address it.

Thank you, Mr. Chairman.

Senator MARKEY. Thank you. I thank the Senators. I thank the panel. This is actually a panel we could not have had 5 years ago. The State Department did not have an Energy Bureau and the Department of Defense and USAID did not nearly as fully integrate climate into any of their strategizing 5 years ago. But the world has changed and we are just trying to be realistic about what is happening out there.

Again, I think that Blackhawk Down in Somalia, with 11 and 12 three- and four-star admirals and generals saying that was the cause, is enough for us to pay close attention to the threats that could emerge in the future. I congratulate President Obama for his focus on this, and we thank this panel for their great work.

I tell you what. I will ask each of you to give us the 30 seconds you want us to remember from your testimony, and that would be I think very helpful to us. So, Mr. Hochstein.

Mr. HOCHSTEIN. I think, just as you said, that the integral interplay of geopolitics and energy security are going to continue to be interwoven and will have effects one on the other. We need to have a clearer and better and deeper understanding of the role that energy is playing in decisionmaking around the world and how that affects our own national security and global national security.

Senator MARKEY. Mr. Postel.

Mr. POSTEL. For USAID, climate variability has the potential to affect our entire portfolio of work on development, affecting billions of people. So we are working hard to try to factor this in and make sure that we are good stewards of taxpayer money with all our investments across the board.

Senator MARKEY. Dr. Chiu.

Dr. CHIU. For DOD, the emphasis I would highlight is on planning for the effects of climate change, not to make predictions, but to be prepared so that we are not caught off guard.

Senator MARKEY. Thank you. Thank you all for your service to our country, and we will take a minute here and just change the name plates and ask for the second panel to move up to the table.

[Pause.]

Senator MARKEY. We welcome the second panel and we have just as distinguished a group on the second panel as was on the first, and the subject deserves it. We are going to begin by recognizing Rear Admiral David Titley, Retired, who is a Board Member of CNA Military Advisory Board. We welcome you, Admiral. Whenever you are ready, please begin.

STATEMENT OF RADM DAVID W. TITLEY, USN [RETIRED], MEMBER, CNA MILITARY ADVISORY BOARD, AND DIRECTOR, CENTER FOR SOLUTIONS TO WEATHER AND CLIMATE RISK, THE PENNSYLVANIA STATE UNIVERSITY, ARLINGTON, VA

Admiral TITLEY. Thank you very much, Mr. Chairman. Chairman Markey, Ranking Member Barrasso, and distinguished members of the subcommittee, thanks for the opportunity to discuss the implications of climate change on geopolitical security. It is a privilege to come before you today and discuss this very important topic.

Before I begin with my oral statement, I would request, sir, that we can submit the MAB report for the record.

Senator MARKEY. Without objection.

[EDITOR'S NOTE.—The MAB report mentioned above was too voluminous to include in the printed hearing. It will be retained in the permanent record of the committee.]

Admiral TITLEY. I am David Titley. I currently serve as a member of CNA's Military Advisory Board, or MAB for short. In this capacity, I am here today not only representing my views on security implications of climate change, but on the collective wisdom of 16 admirals and generals who also serve on CNA's MAB. I am also the director for the Center for Solutions to Weather and Climate Risk at the Pennsylvania State University.

I had the honor of serving in the United States Navy for 32 years, where my capstone assignment was Oceanographer and Navigator of the Navy, and under ADM Gary Roughead's direction, I assumed leadership of the U.S. Navy's Task Force on Climate Change.

Sir, our collective bottom-line judgment is that climate change is an accelerating risk to our Nation's future. Although we have seen some movement in climate mitigation and adaptation, the MAB felt compelled to issue our latest report because of the lack of sufficient comprehensive action by both the United States and the international community. Strengthening resilience to climate impacts is critical, but to ultimately reduce the long-term risk, we must take action to stabilize the climate.

Climate does not change in a vacuum. It impacts and in turn is affected by our food, energy, and most of all water demands. The world has added over half a billion people since our first climate report in 2007 and increasingly people are moving to coastal urban areas, where the impacts of a changing climate and sea level rise will be the greatest. We will deal with all of this in a very fiscally constrained environment. Failure to think about how climate change might impact our globally interconnected systems and all elements of U.S. power and security is, frankly, a failure of imagination.

If there is a canary in the climate coal mine, if I can mix my metaphors, it is the Arctic. Arguably, there has been no region on Earth where the climate has changed faster in recent decades than the Arctic. Those changes are making the region more accessible to a wide variety of human activities, including shipping, resource extraction, fishing, and tourism.

While the MAB is encouraged to see U.S. policymakers planning for the Arctic and for climate change in general—the 2014 Department of Defense Quadrennial Defense Review, U.S. Navy's recently updated Arctic Road Map, and the Senate's Fiscal Year 2015 Defense Appropriations Act report are all good examples of that—the MAB does believe that the United States and the international community could accelerate continued development of Arctic capacity and capability to match the speed of observed changes in that critical region.

Climate change will affect our military in very real ways, by creating new mission sets, just as I discussed with the Arctic, by placing our bases under stress from sea level rise, droughts, floods, wildfires, and heat stress, and by stretching overall capacity by adding additional domestic disaster relief missions to our guard forces at a time when we are downsizing our ground forces.

Mr. Chairman, we know you understand these changes and their risks. As you already mentioned in your opening statement, 7 years ago when you were a Member of the U.S. House, General Sullivan, then chair of the MAB, testified before your committee about the impact of climate and drought in Somalia and the cascading effect of poor governance, famine, forced migration, and the consequences that we only, frankly, understood in hindsight.

I wish I could tell you today that such weather and climate-related impacts were an aberration. Unfortunately, my professional assessment, along with that of my MAB colleagues, is that these increasingly serious impacts to our security will only continue to increase in both frequency and consequence barring meaningful action to both adapt to the changes in climate and ultimately to stabilize a system on which mankind has literally built civilization.

ADM Skip Bowman, fellow MAB member and former Director of Naval Reactors, shared with us his key tenets. They are: face the facts; respect even small amounts of risk, especially when that risk has large consequence; seek total responsibility; and require continually rising performance. I believe Admiral Bowman's tenets are an excellent framework to think through not only the planning, but the required actions needed to adapt to and stabilize the climate.

In closing, Senator, the potential security ramifications of global climate change should serve as catalysts for cooperation and change. Instead, climate change impacts are already accelerating instability in vulnerable areas of the world and are serving as catalysts for conflict. We believe, though, that continued leadership and tangible pragmatic actions of the United States are critical to minimizing the worst outcomes and maximizing our opportunities for a better world.

I will be happy to take your questions, sir.

[The prepared statement of Admiral Titley follows:]

PREPARED STATEMENT BY RADM (RET.) DAVID W. TITLEY

Chairman Markey, Ranking Member Barrasso, and distinguished members of the committee, thank you for the opportunity to discuss the implications of climate change on geopolitical security. It is a privilege to come before you today and discuss this very important topic.

INTRODUCTION

I am David Titley and I currently serve as the Director of the Center for Solutions to Weather and Climate Risk at the Pennsylvania State University. I had the honor of serving in the United States Navy for 32 years where my capstone assignment was Oceanographer and Navigator of the Navy, Director of U.S. Navy Task Force Climate Change, and Assistant Deputy Chief of Naval Operations for Information Dominance. Subsequent to my time in the Navy, I served as Chief Operating Officer at the National Oceanic and Atmospheric Administration (NOAA).

My Center at Penn State currently receives no Federal funding and my views do not necessarily represent those of the Pennsylvania State University.

You invited me here today in my position as a member of CNA's Military Advisory Board—MAB for short. In this capacity I am here today not only representing my views on the security implications of climate change, but the collective wisdom of the 16 Admirals and Generals who also serve on CNA's MAB.

I. Global Trends: Accelerating Risks

Since we published our first report in 2007 on the national security implications of climate change, we have witnessed nearly a decade of scientific discoveries in environmental science, burgeoning scholarly literature on complex global interdependence associated with climate change, and a series of reactions, or in many cases failure to react, to the impacts of climate change. In the 7 years that have passed since our initial assessment we have witnessed more frequent and/or intense weather events, including heat waves, sustained heavy downpours, floods in some regions, and droughts in others areas. Nine of the ten costliest storms to hit the United States have occurred in the past 10 years, including Hurricane Katrina and Superstorm Sandy. Speaking for the MAB, we assess that the nature and pace of observed climate changes—and an emerging scientific consensus on their projected consequences—pose severe risks for our national security. Still, there those who remain skeptical about the observed changes, the causes, and debate on the magnitude of the risk.

When I was on Active Duty, both serving as the Senior Military Assistant to the Direcot of Net Assessment and particularly as a Flag Officer was how to think about risk and uncertainty. Managing risk is seldom about dealing with absolute certainties but, rather, involves careful analysis of the probability of an event and the consequences should the event occur. When it comes to our national security, even very low probability events with dire consequences must be considered and mitigation/adaptation schemes developed and employed. Rather than assessing a range of estimates as proof of disagreement that can be used to justify inaction, military leaders view such evidence through the lens of varying degrees of risk the estimates could represent. Military leaders evaluate the probability and possible consequences of events in determining overall risk. Today, the risks posed by predicted climate change, in the MAB's judgment, represent even graver potential than they did 7 years ago and require action today to reduce risk tomorrow.

A. Four important global trends

There are four import global trends, worthy of note, which will provide additional fuel to the accelerating risks of climate change. First is global population growth. Half a billion people have been added since the MAB completed its first report in 2007 and another half billion will be added by 2025. Most of this growth is in Africa and Asia, two of the areas likely to be most impacted by climate change. The second trend is urbanization. Nearly half of the world now lives in urban areas with 16 out of 20 of the largest urban areas being near coastlines. The result is more of the world's population is at risk from extreme weather events and sea level rise. The next trend is a global increase in the middle class with an accompanying growth in demand for food, water, and energy. The National Intelligence Community predicts that by 2030 demand for food would increase by 35 percent, fresh water by 40 percent, and energy 50 percent. Even without the climate changing, it will be a challenge to meet these growth targets. Climate change will further stress the world's ability to produce food and drinkable water at levels necessary to meet demand. A 2012 National Intelligence Council assessment found that water challenges will likely increase the risk of instability and state failure, exacerbate regional tensions, and divert attention from working with the United States and other key allies on important policy objectives. The final trend notes that the world is becoming more politically complex and economically and financially interdependent. As such, we believe it is no longer adequate to think of the projected climate impacts to any one region of the world in isolation. Climate change impacts, combined with globalization, transcend international borders and geographic areas of responsibility.

B. Accelerating risks around the world affect U.S. National Security

The world around us is changing. In recent years we have observed changing weather patterns manifest by prolonged drought in some areas and heavier precipitation in others. In the last few years we have seen unprecedented wildfires threaten homes, habitats, and food supplies, not only across the United States, but also across Australia, Europe, Central Russia, and China. Low-lying island nations are preparing for complete evacuation to escape rising sea levels. Globally, we have seen recent prolonged drought act as a factor driving both spikes in food prices and mass displacement of populations, each contributing to instability and eventual conflict. For example in Syria, 5 years of drought decimated farms and forced millions to migrate to urban areas. In overpopulated cities, these climate refugees found little in the way of jobs and were quickly disenfranchised with the government. The ongoing strife in Syria has been exacerbated by drought and rural to urban migration. In this way climate change has exacerbated a region already torn by political and ethnic tensions, serving as a catalyst for conflict. Over the coming decades we are concerned about the projected impacts of climate change on those areas already stressed by water and food shortage and poor governance—these span the globe, but present the greatest short-term threat. In the longer term it is those areas that will be threatened by rising sea level that are most at risk. There will be only so much we can do to keep the sea out, and in some areas the sea will not flow over the walls we build, it will flow under or around and make the land and aquifers not useable. We are concerned about low lying islands in the Pacific and great deltas including the Mekong, the delta of Bangladesh, the Nile delta in Egypt, the Mississippi delta and whole regions like the Everglades. Seawater inundation will drastically cut food production in many of these areas and cause millions to lose their ability to live on these retreating areas. Migration will become a larger form of adaptation. We will need to learn how to accept large transnational migration of people peacefully.

II. Accelerating Climate Risks to the U.S. Homeland

A. Arctic is rapidly changing—U.S. needs to prepare

While all of the areas of increased population, stresses on food and water resource are of growing concern, one of the areas about which we have the greatest immediate concern is the Arctic. Over the past few years, we have seen an almost exponential rise in the activity in the Arctic; more shipping, more resource extraction and more posturing for control over the resources. The Arctic is an example of where climate change should serve as a catalyst for international cooperation. The world is not yet prepared to respond to an accident or disaster that could occur with increasing shipping and energy exploration in this fragile region with limited infrastructure and extreme operating conditions. Some great work has been done across the U.S. Government in putting together plans for increased future operation in the Arctic, with the Navy's 2014 Arctic Roadmap as one example. The challenge is that the increase is happening now. Seventy-three ships sailed through the Northwest Passage in 2013, up from 4 in 2007; meanwhile the Russians planted a flag on the sea bottom near the North Pole. Preparations for energy exploration are well underway. We assess that today we do not have the communications equipment, navigation aids, and sufficient ice hardened ships to respond to natural or manmade disasters in that fragile area or to protect our vital interests. In other words, we are not prepared in the short term for the rate of increase and we must invest today in increasing our capability and capacity.

B. Growing awareness of climate risks and planning in the U.S.

On the positive side, we have seen increased awareness of climate risks in communities around the U.S., and constructive planning underway in various regions, regardless of whether the state or region is ''red'' or ''blue.'' Two examples are worth noting.

The first example is Hampton Roads, Virginia, where the military and the local community are jointly addressing sea level rise. Rising sea levels, natural subsidence, and storms pose risks to the many military facilities, related commercial shipyards, and community in this critically important region. The area has hundreds of miles of waterfront from three major rivers that flow into the Chesapeake Bay. The DOD realizes that sea level rise will affect both the Hampton Roads installations and the surrounding civilian community. DOD, working with other Federal, State, and local agencies, as well as the Climate Change and Sea Level Rise Institute at Old Dominion University has launched an aggressive effort to develop plans and measures to sustain the vital missions of this region and protect the surrounding communities. Our report specifically highlights the initiatives of the Hampton Road area as a positive case study.

Second, and very recently, the Pensacola Florida region is considering how to build and rebuild in a future climate that is very different than what we experience today. Spurred on by the historic floods this past April as well as the projections in the National Climate Assessment, many scientists, citizens and government leaders in the Pensacola area understand that the time to act is now, and that prudent planning and preparation will save lives, money, and economic opportunities in the long run.

III. Increasing Impacts on Military Readiness

Along with planning for increased Arctic operations, the MAB was pleased to see that the changing climate is reflected throughout the 2014 Defense Department Quadrennial Defense Review (QDR). The MAB holds that projected climate change will have three major impacts on the military: more demand; challenges to readiness; and new and harsher operating environments.

The MAB expects to see an increased demand for forces across the full spectrum of operations. Domestically, response to extreme weather events and wildfires in the U.S. will increase demand for National Guard, and Reserves. The frequency, severity, and probability that these events may happen simultaneously will also likely increase demand for Active Duty Forces to provide defense support for civilian authority (DSCA). This causes us concern because, in a leaner military, many of our capabilities reside in the Guard and Reserve and if they are being used domestically they are less available to respond to worldwide crisis. We saw this impact following tropical storm Sandy.

Globally there will be increased demand for humanitarian response and disaster relief in response to extreme weather. Witness more than 13,000 military troops that responded to Typhoon Haiyan in the Philippines late last year. As importantly, climate change will be a catalyst for conflict in fragile areas and U.S. military involvement could be an option in response to the conflicts.

In addition to more demand, which in itself will stress readiness, our bases will be increasingly at risk from the effects of climate change. Our bases are where we generate readiness. It is where we train, garrison, repair, maintain and prepare to deploy. Our bases are vulnerable to sea level rise, extreme weather including drought, which restricts training because of the threat of wildfire, and in the future increased precipitation in the form of rain and snow may limit training. It is not just the bases, but also the surrounding communities, which house and support the military. If our sailors, soldiers airmen and marines can't get to the base because the road is flooded then we can't generate readiness.

Finally, climate change will cause the military to be deployed to harsher environments. Higher temperatures will stress equipment and people, while at the same time the opening of the Arctic present a whole new set of challenges where the military will be expected to respond to everything from search and rescue, to disasters (weather and man-made) to resolution of conflict and protection of vital interests.

IV. National Power Affected by Climate Risks

The final area I want to cover is how climate change will impact the elements of national power, here at home.

National security is more than just having a strong or capable military. American's security is determined by multiple elements of national power: diplomacy, information, military and economic, at a minimum. When deployed strategically, they can constitute ''smart power.'' On the vulnerability side, National Power can also be assessed by degradations to a nation's political, military, economic, social, infrastructure, and information systems. The MAB has addressed how projected climate change could degrade our National Power and particularly focused on military, infrastructure, economic, and social support systems.

Strain on Military Readiness and Base Resiliency. As discussed earlier, the projected impacts of climate change could be detrimental to military readiness, strain base resilience both at home and abroad, and may limit our ability to respond to future demands. The projected impacts of climate change will strain our military forces in the coming decades. More forces will be called on to respond in the wake of extreme weather events at home and abroad, limiting their ability to respond to other contingencies. Projected climate change will make training more difficult, while at the same time, putting at greater risk critical military logistics, transportation systems, and infrastructure, both on and off base.

Risks to Critical Infrastructure. The impacts of projected climate change can be detrimental to the physical components of our national critical infrastructure, while also limiting their capacities.

The Nation depends on critical infrastructure for economic prosperity, safety, and the essentials of everyday life. Projected climate change will impact all 16 critical infrastructure sectors identified in Homeland Security planning directives. We are already seeing how extreme heat is damaging the national transportation infrastructure such as roads, rail lines, and airport runways. We also note that much of the Nation's energy infrastructure—including oil and gas refineries, storage tanks, power plants, and electricity transmission lines—are located in coastal floodplains, where they are increasingly threatened by more intense storms, extreme flooding, and rising sea levels. Projected increased temperatures and drought across much of the nation will strain energy systems with more demand for cooling, possibly dislocate and reduce food production, and result in water scarcity. Since much of the critical infrastructure is owned or operated by the private sector, government solutions alone will not be able to address the full range of climate-related challenges.

Economic Costs. The projected impacts of climate change will threaten major sections of the U.S. economy.

According to the 2014 National Climate Assessment, ''The observed warming and other climatic changes are triggering wide-ranging impacts in every region of our country and throughout our economy. . . .'' Most of the U.S. economic sectors, including international trade, will be negatively affected by projected climate change. Major storms, such as Superstorm Sandy, cost the U.S. an estimated $50 billion in damages.

On the other hand, as we recognize these risks, communities such as New York and New Jersey are adapting and making this region more resilient to extreme events in the future.

Local Communities Affected Too. The projected impacts of climate change will affect major sections of our society and stress social support systems such as first responders. As coastal regions become increasingly populated and developed, more frequent or severe storms will threaten vulnerable populations in these areas and increase the requirements for emergency responders in terms of frequency and severity of storms. Simultaneous or widespread extreme weather events and/or wildfires, accompanied by mass evacuations, and degraded critical infrastructure could outstrip local and Federal Government resources, and require the increased use of military and private sector support.

CONCLUSION

The time for action is NOW. Projected climate change may cause increased instability around the world; we are not prepared for the pace of climate change as evidenced by our lack of capability and capacity to respond to the opening of the Arctic; climate change will likely impact our military readiness and support systems as well as cause increased demand for forces, both at home and abroad, and finally climate change will impact elements of our national power here at home. Let me leave you with these comments by my fellow MAB General and Flag Officers:

> At the end of the day, we validate the findings of our first report and find that in many cases the risks we identified are advancing noticeably faster than we anticipated. We also find the world becoming more complex in terms of the problems that plague its various regions. Yet thinking about climate change as just a regional problem or—worse yet—someone else's problem may limit the ability to fully understand its consequences and cascading effects. We see more clearly now that while projected climate change should serve as catalyst for change and cooperation, it can also be a catalyst for conflict. We are dismayed that discussions of climate change have become so polarizing and have receded from the arena of informed public discourse and debate. Political posturing and budgetary woes cannot be allowed to inhibit discussion and debate over what so many believe to be a salient national security concern for our Nation.

In their forward to the CNA MAB report, former Secretary of Defense Panetta and former Secretary of Homeland Security Michael Chertoff summarized our most important message for the committee: ''The update serves as a bipartisan call to action. It makes a compelling case that climate change is no longer a future threat—it is taking place now. . . . actions to build resilience against the project impacts of climate are required today. We no longer have the option to wait and see.''

Thank you for your attention and focus on what is one of the most important issues to our Nation's future security and well-being.

Senator MARKEY. Thank you, Admiral, very much.

Our next witness, Mr. David Goldwyn, is a nonresident senior fellow at the Energy Security Initiative at the Brookings Institution. Welcome, sir.

STATEMENT OF DAVID L. GOLDWYN, NONRESIDENT SENIOR FELLOW, ENERGY SECURITY INITIATIVE AT THE BROOKINGS INSTITUTION, WASHINGTON, DC

Mr. GOLDWYN. Thank you, Mr. Chairman, Mr. Ranking Member. I will summarize my statement. I would be grateful if the full statement was entered into the record.

It is really an honor for me to talk to you today about the foreign policy challenges facing the United States and how we can respond to protect both energy security and climate change. We really face even historically an unprecedented amount of uncertainty in energy markets. We are looking at supply disruptions in Iraq, possibly Russia, Nigeria, Sudan, and Venezuela. We have policy risks. Things could go either way with negotiations with Iran and with Russia, which could lead to significant displacement of supply or increased supply. And as many of my fellow panelists have talked about, the growing risk of conflict driven by climate change.

We have a lot of tools at our disposal to address these risks. One of them is helping ourselves through our own production. As Amos Hochstein said, our ability to grow our production has helped mitigate that nearly 3 million barrels a day in displaced oil that conflict has presented the global economy. The fact that we have increased gas production has allowed LNG supplies to flow to other countries, which has decreased the cost for them and decreased Russia's revenues.

The question is whether we are doing all that we can, with all the tools that we have, to mitigate the risks that we are facing today. The four key tools that we have are: first, energy diplomacy, and that really means policy reform, talking to other countries about how to get prices right so energy efficiency and other technologies can be deployed.

The second is technical assistance, helping countries grow their own supplies, whether it is oil, gas, or renewables, or how to introduce tariffs that will allow renewable energy into their electricity systems.

The third is the promotion of deep and liquid energy markets. Part of that is the fourth tool, which is exports, which is how do we connect our providence to the global economy in a way that can reduce prices and increase availability overall. I think that we can deploy all these tools in a way that both reduces greenhouse gas emissions and increases energy security by giving other countries access to lower carbon resources, whether those are natural gas or renewables or some combination of the two, or coal with carbon sequestration.

So to give an example, in Ukraine the number one job we have, as Senator Murphy said earlier, is getting prices right. No one wants to buy energy efficiency equipment unless you are saving money. You cannot save money if the price is below the cost of the electricity itself. So getting prices right is job one. Growing their own supply is probably job two. Diversifying their supply and having more energy storage is job three. So there is a lot that we can do with Ukraine to help them get access to more diverse supplies.

Europe overall, we need the entire suite. Europe needs an integrated gas market so you can move LNG from Spain all the way to Ukraine. They do not have that right now. They need to reduce monopolies and enforce antitrust laws so that Gazprom does not own all the infrastructure inside of Europe. They need to provide more LNG access so they can access more gas. They need better interconnections, they need indigenous gas, they need to rethink nuclear European as well.

Even in the Caribbean and Central America—I made reference in my testimony to a report I put out with the Atlantic Council last week which talks about the ways that the Caribbean and Central America can get off of fuel oil and diesel, reduce their electricity costs, reduce their carbon footprint, by accessing natural gas, because they will get to renewables, but they have serious policy obstacles.

So we could make the cheapest natural gas available, which comes from the U.S. gulf coast, enable them to cut their costs in half, be more competitive, and address our own security challenges as well.

So in nearly every case we can add to our own security by signaling that we will be helpful with supply as well. We can do policy reform, we can do technical assistance, but the reality is is that we have natural gas in abundance and we have certain grades of crude

oil in abundance as well, light oil that we need less and condensates that we need less than we need heavy oil. And simply by
signaling that we will make those supplies available to the global
market, we can help impact price formation, and by impacting
price formation we can make the cost of that lower carbon energy
more accessible, whether that is cheaper European for Ukraine,
whether that is cheaper natural gas for the Caribbean, or whether
that is even easier gas access for parts of Africa that are now using
diesel or fuel oil or even biomass.

So I think there are things that we can do. I do not profess that
it is a simple question, but I think there are a lot of studies going
on. Right now there have been many on LNG, some going on crude
oil which show that we can do this without impacting domestic
prices and we can manage the climate impacts as well.

So all I would say now is that we should take energy security
and climate security with equal seriousness, that we need to look
at the options about how we can advance both of these agendas.
I think there are options that involve diplomacy, that involve technical assistance, and that involve more competitive markets, and I
would just urge the committee to give all of them a fair hearing.

Thank you.

[The prepared statement of Mr. Goldwyn follows:]

PREPARED STATEMENT OF DAVID L. GOLDWYN

Mr. Chairman and members of the subcommittee, it is an honor to speak with
you today about challenges to U.S. national security interests and their impact on
both our energy security and climate change. We are experiencing a period of great
instability in the world's major energy producing regions. We have been able to mitigate the impacts of this instability due largely to unprecedented growth in U.S. and
more broadly North American energy supply. Going forward we will need to use a
variety of tools to enhance our security, including promotion of competitive energy
markets, advocacy of energy policy reform in other countries, technical assistance
to help countries produce their own energy and promotion of energy exports. I
believe we can harmonize our interests in mitigating global climate change—
a national security risk itself—and advancing our energy security. In many cases
the alternative sources of energy supply the United States should promote are lower
in carbon than those that vulnerable countries rely on today. In Europe, in the Caribbean and Central America, in Africa and elsewhere, the U.S. can make lower carbon energy, especially natural gas, more available and affordable, through effective
diplomacy and promotion of open markets.

CHALLENGES TO U.S. NATIONAL SECURITY

The national security challenges the United States faces across the globe have inherent energy components. The most prominent issues include the threat posed by
Iran's nuclear program, continued Russian efforts to foment instability in Ukraine,
the emergence of the Islamic State of Iraq and the Levant (ISIL) as a destabilizing
force in Syria and Iraq, continued instability in North Africa, and the recent accel-
eration of the Israeli-Palestinian conflict. These are conflicts involving a great percentage of the world's major energy suppliers. We face additional challenges to the
stability of Central America and the Caribbean, as Venezuela's economic deterioration puts its ability to provide credit support for regional energy purchases through
Petrocaribe at increasing risk. Energy poverty in Africa and South Asia pose risks
to stability in those regions. The way in which each of these issues is managed or
resolved has implications for global energy markets and by extension our own economic growth and prosperity.

Climate change itself poses a significant risk to national security. The Pentagon's
Quadrennial Defense Review, released in March 2014, identifies climate change as
a threat multiplier capable of exacerbating poverty, environmental degradation, political instability, and social tensions—all of which contribute to terrorist activity
and other forms of violence.[1] A report issued by the government-funded CNA Military Advisory Board, released in May 2014, drew similar conclusions and discussed,

among other issues, the contributions of climate-induced drought toward fomenting regional and ethnic tensions in the Middle East and Africa.[2]

The U.S. has multiple tools at its disposal to mitigate the impacts of energy supply disruptions, help countries enhance their own energy security and mitigate global climate change. In ''Energy and Security: Strategies for a World in Transition,'' a book that I coedited and was published last year, we argue that these tools include using diplomacy to advocate policy reform, providing technical assistance to other nations to help propagate the unconventional oil and gas revolution abroad, and promoting deep and competitive energy markets by embracing energy exports as means of making energy more affordable and accessible to friends and allies.[3]

Energy diplomacy

As in every area of foreign policy, diplomacy is our first line of defense. Diplomacy is the means by which we produced multilateral sanctions to bring Iran to the negotiating table. It will also be required to keep Iraq from fragmenting, and facilitating unity among stakeholders so that ISIS is repelled and Iraq's contribution to global energy supply is sustained. In many regions the U.S. needs to advocate for the policy reforms required to attract energy investment, reduce subsidies, reduce dependency on a single fuel or supplier or open markets to U.S. exports or investment. The new Energy Bureau at the State Department that I helped to design when I served under Secretary Clinton has a leading role in this mission. One of the best historical examples of this work is U.S. policy on European energy security. Over the past two decades the U.S. has been more vigorous in advocating the need for Europe to have an integrated gas market, more energy storage, more diverse production, and stronger antitrust policy. The U.S. has shared advancements we made in energy efficiency and renewable energy with Europe, including building and appliance standards that have helped Europe greatly diversify its energy supply base and better weather Russian gas supply interruptions.

Technical assistance

The U.S. can also help other countries grow their own energy supply through technical assistance. Two examples of this are all of government programs led by Department of State Bureau of Energy Resources (ENR): the Unconventional Gas Technical Engagement Program (UGTEP) and the Energy Governance and Capacity Initiative (EGCI). UGTEP takes many forms, from U.S. Geological Survey resource assessments to help countries understand if they have recoverable resources, to visitor programs where country delegations can meet with Federal, State and local regulators to understand how to protect air, water, and land and see first hand how an operation looks on the ground. The EGCI program helps countries considering energy development avoid the resource curse by teaching their Central Banks and Finance Ministries how to manage the income from energy production, while teaching their petroleum ministries how to understand their resource base, and use licensing to protect the environment.

Competitive markets and free trade

A major pillar of American foreign policy since the Second World War has been the promotion of open markets to promote economic growth and bind nations together. We have worked for decades to encourage those with resources—oil, gas, coal or rare earth materials, to produce what they can, use what they need, and make the rest available for trade. We have benefited enormously from this system whenever we needed imports of energy, and commodities flowed easily and efficiently to our shores in times of crisis, like the days after Hurricanes Rita and Katrina. We fight against restrictions on rare earth minerals in the WTO to ensure that energy efficient products can be produced and then made available to the global market.

For the U.S. today this means that our contribution to our own energy security and that of the planet is to produce our own energy, use what we need and export the balance. For our own sake we need to produce our own new resources with safety and the environment as top priorities. All companies—including the smaller independents—need a strong safety culture, from ensuring well bore integrity in deepwater or deep shale beds, to securing the safe disposal of water produced from ''tight'' hydrocarbon plays.

But the reality is that, we can dramatically enhance our own security and that of others by connecting ourselves to the global market we have spend decades developing and benefiting from. First, we can enhance our own prosperity. The United States and other stable, democratic countries, such as Canada and Australia, are well poised to meet a considerable share of the world's growing oil and gas demand and attain the associated export revenues. From a geopolitical perspective, increased LNG exports from the U.S. and its allies would shift rents away from traditional, autocratic suppliers, including Russia, that have used the proceeds to finance policies at odds with U.S. national security interests. U.S. supply also promotes price competition and stability in global oil and gas markets. Price stability benefits U.S. economic growth, and also better ensures that U.S. adversaries that are major oil and gas exporters are less able to enjoy higher export revenues stemming from major global supply disruptions. Numerous studies have shown the U.S. enjoys net benefits from exports, with minimal domestic price impacts from LNG exports and potential decreases in domestic gasoline prices from crude oil exports.[4]

Second, building a more competitive LNG market can help mitigate global climate change. In the coming decades, the greatest risk of greenhouse gas emissions growth comes from non-OECD Asia, which is forecast to account for 65 percent of total energy demand growth through 2035. China and India alone are expected to build nearly 40 percent of the world's new generation capacity, and both countries are currently heavily reliant on coal as a base load fuel.[5] While work on creating commercial scale carbon sequestration continues, the best way to address emission growth is to help these countries meet incremental demand through lower carbon alternatives. These alternative sources need to be able to supply base load electricity supply at scale. The currently available, scalable options are petroleum products such as fuel oil or diesel, nuclear power, and natural gas. Petroleum products are an inefficient, expensive and high carbon means of electricity generation. Nuclear energy is a complex technology, and safe infrastructure takes over a decade to build.

U.S. LNG exports help make gas more affordable for Europe and Asia where, unlike the U.S., natural gas is now much more expensive than coal. U.S. natural gas production has already lowered global LNG prices by displacing supplies meant for the U.S. market. The increased availability of natural gas on global energy markets from future LNG exports makes it increasingly cost effective for the largest emerging energy consumers, including China and India, to convert their electric power infrastructure to natural gas. The growing adoption of natural gas as a fuel for electricity generation in the Chinese and Indian markets would render considerable positive climate impacts. It would also have a multiplier effect, as increased adoption of natural gas by these large energy consumers would leave smaller yet still important consumers better positioned to attain financing of their own to build or convert infrastructure to accommodate more natural gas in their own energy mixes.

Natural gas thus remains the obvious fuel choice to serve as a bridge to scalable renewable energy. While we should continue to pursue a future with abundant use of renewable energy, renewables will not be able to be adopted for grid based systems at scale in the developing world until the battery storage challenge is addressed. Ensuring that renewables are significant source of longer term supply, and embracing natural gas as a bridge fuel to cut emissions now, are not mutually exclusive goals. Even at their current limited scalability, the U.S. should support efforts to integrate renewables into the energy mix where they are viable. Additionally, the fact that most energy demand growth is expected to come from the non-OECD does not absolve the U.S. from embracing policies that will reduce our own carbon emissions. Indeed, U.S. efforts to lead by example and in cooperation with our allies are likely to facilitate more international buy-in of such policies.

MEETING OUR CURRENT CHALLENGES

We will need to use all the tools in our tool kit to meet the energy and security challenges we face today.

Ukraine

The most obvious national security challenge where energy security issues are explicitly at play is Russia's continued aggression in Ukraine. Russia continues to lend material support to separatists operating in Eastern Ukraine and last month stopped supplying natural gas to Kiev. While this is yet to bring about a critical gas shortage in Europe or Ukraine, there are justifiable fears that such shortages will ensue if the Russian cutoff persists into this winter, when the seasonal heating period begins and demand increases considerably.[6]

The U.S. needs to use diplomacy, technical assistance and support exports to help not only the the efforts of Ukraine, but also other countries proximate to Russia, including those in Western Europe, to diversify their sources of supply. The diplomatic agenda is pressing for a divided Europe to finish the work of integrating its gas market, promoting internal market reform in member countries, developing further infrastructure to support alternative gas supplies and interconnections among member countries, and encouraging indigenous gas development. However, there is also ample space where the United States has and can continue to provide assistance. In the past the U.S. promoted infrastructure projects, such as the Baku- Tbilisi-Ceyhan and the Southern corridor. More recently the U.S., led by the ENR Bureau, has advocated ''reverse flows'' of gas, including from Europe to Ukraine. Earlier this month Slovak gas pipeline operator Eustream indicated that it would have a route transiting EU gas to Ukraine running at full capacity before the winter heating season begins. Reverse flows are also reaching Ukraine from both Poland and Hungary.[7] Additionally, ENR, under the auspices of both UGTEP and EGCI, has engaged with countries in the region on potential paths forward in developing their shale resources to boost their domestic energy production and provide new regional sources of supply. This advocacy should be elevated to higher levels.

Export policy can help as well. A clear signal from the U.S. that LNG exports will be available to European allies for future purchase would put immediate pressure on Russia's market share and export revenues, and would also provide a market signal to help accelerate investment in, and construction of, gas transportation infrastructure in Europe. The new policy change suggested by the Department of Energy for considering LNG exports should help provide certainty to the market in this regard.[8] Price expectations matter. The U.S. shale boom, through freeing up LNG cargoes originally destined for the U.S. to instead reach Europe, has already put downward pressure on European gas prices. These developments contributed to the increased leverage that Gazprom's European customers have enjoyed in recent years, enabling them to renegotiate contracts for the purchase of natural gas from Gazprom to their advantage. While many skeptics question whether Europe would receive U.S. LNG due to the expected higher prices in Asian markets, the fact remains that European prices could easily approach Asian levels in the event of a Russian supply cutoff. Additionally, purchasers consider not only price, but also the diversity of supply source and the likelihood of timely project completion, which may leave at least some European purchasers predisposed to paying a premium price for U.S. gas that rivals the market price Asian purchasers are willing to pay.[9]

A robust U.S. market share in the Asian gas market offers geopolitical advantages to the United States, and has positive implications for the future of our climate, as well.

Iraq

Geopolitical tensions also continue to plague the Middle East, as the Islamic State of Iraq and the Levant's (ISIL) takeover of large shares of territory in western Iraq marks the first major spillover of the Syrian civil war that threatens the free flow of oil from the region. To date, the violence has not affected Iraq's key export infrastructure, which is located in the heavily Shiite far south of the country. But the July 20 ISIS takeover of gas fields in Syria and its efforts to gain control of the Baiji refinery in Iraq signal its intent to disrupt energy infrastructure. Iraq's geography does not entirely mitigate the risk of a supply disruption. Violence in the far south could induce international companies to pull out larger shares of their foreign personnel, which would have negative implications for Iraqi production.

The U.S. approach in Iraq should primarily comprise efforts to foster reconciliation among Iraqi stakeholders. Yet the U.S. should also be prepared to continue supporting the stability of the global oil market should a supply disruption occur. U.S. domestic production growth has helped keep the global market well supplied and prices stable even as unplanned supply disruptions, including in places like Libya, South Sudan, and Yemen, have emerged.[10] However, the U.S. could do more, including taking steps to authorize the export of light sweet crude grades that we have in excess, to help keep the global market stable. While promoting global market stability is among the goals of strategic reserves, the United States does not need to tap the Strategic Petroleum Reserve at this time. Instead, it only needs to signal very clearly that it is prepared to export grades of excess crude if disruptions worsen and the global market requires more supply. Numerous studies emerging this fall, including one from Brookings to be released this September, will closely examine the impacts of such action on the U.S. economy.

Central America and the Caribbean

One major opportunity the U.S. has to promote regional security and climate change mitigation is in our own neighborhood. Last week the Atlantic Council published a report [11] I authored on the Caribbean region's dependence on Petrocaribe, a Venezuelan-backed program that allows cash-strapped Caribbean and Central American countries to purchase Venezuelan crude oil and petroleum products on generous financing terms. While this program once provided these countries with immediate-term budget support, it left them increasingly indebted to Venezuela, and reliant on high-carbon, expensive fuel oil and diesel for electricity generation. The high cost of this fuel has made these economies uncompetitive: a recent Inter-American Development Bank Study [12] found that the average retail tariff for 10 major Caribbean utilities in 2012 at \$0.33 per kilowatt-hour, compared to \$0.10 across all sectors of the U.S. in April 2014.[13]

A recent IDB Pre-Feasibility Study found that replacing liquid fuels with natural gas, in combination with energy efficiency and renewable energy measures, produced net benefits to every surveyed Caribbean country, lowering the cost of fuel and the price of power, as well as substantially reducing carbon emissions. We recommended that the U.S. build on Vice President Biden's recent visit to the region, and its Caribbean Energy Security Initiative (CESI), by expanding CESI to promote credit incentives to attract investment to make natural gas a more considerable share of the Caribbean's shorter- and medium-term energy mix. The IDB study determined that U.S. Gulf Coast LNG was the cheapest form of delivery, and that small-scale regasification technology could provide every country with appropriate infrastructure at a reasonable long-term cost.

These findings suggest that the U.S. could facilitate a natural gas bridge in the Caribbean by providing credit enhancements through CESI and declaring LNG exports to all Caribbean nations reliant on Petrocaribe, with the exception of Cuba, to be in the national interest. This would contribute to facilitating the marketing of supply to these nations. U.S. LNG is in close proximity to the Caribbean market, and will be cost competitive.

Promoting the adoption of gas in the Caribbean and Central American energy mix would bring about several benefits for U.S. interests. The risk of harm to the region's economies from a Venezuelan interruption of credit support would decrease. Electricity costs for industrial and residential consumers would decline as cheaper natural gas replaces more expensive fuel oil and diesel for electricity generation. Finally, cleaner burning natural gas would reduce the region's carbon footprint.

CONCLUSION

The acknowledgement that national security and climate security concerns are inherently linked is a crucial development for the evolution of U.S. policy both at home and in the national security sphere. This strategic conception of the problems we face should provide policymakers with space to develop policies that maximize global energy supply, promote low-carbon sources, support price stability, and provide our allies and partners with secure sources of supply, either through global markets or their own domestic production, to ensure that their energy security is not at the mercy of a single supplier.

I believe that Congress also has a role to play in accelerating the leveling of the energy playing field. Congress can support the State Department's role in energy diplomacy, expand our technical assistance programs, and consider thoughtfully the role of energy exports in advancing energy security and promoting access to lower carbon fuels.

End Notes

[1] "Quadrennial Defense Review 2014," United States Department of Defense, March 2014, p. 8.

[2] "National Security and the Accelerating Risks of Climate Change," CNA Military Advisory Board, May 2014.

[3] Jan H. Kalicki and David L. Goldwyn, "Energy and Security: Strategies for a World in Transition," Woodrow Wilson Center Press and Johns Hopkins University Press, 2013 (Kalicki and Goldwyn, 2013).

[4] W. David Montgomery, Robert Baron, Paul Bernstein, Sugandha D. Tuladhar, Shirley Xiong and Mei Yuan, "Macroeconomic Impacts of LNG Exports from the United States," NERA Economic Consulting, December 2012; Daniel Yergin, Kurt Barrow, James Fallon, Mohsen Bonakdarpour, Sandeep Sayal, Curtis Smith and Jamie Webster, "U.S. Crude Oil Export Decision: Assessing the impact of the export ban and free trade on the U.S. economy," IHS Global Insight, May 2014.

[5] "World Energy Outlook 2013," International Energy Agency, November, 2013.

[6] Peggy Hollinger, Christian Oliver, and Jack Farchy, "Europe risks 'significant' gas shortages this winter," Financial Times, July 11, 2014.

[7] Tim Gosling, "Slovak gas link to give Ukraine 'chance of lasting through the winter'," Financial Times, July 8, 2014.

[8] For more information about this issue see: David L. Goldwyn, "DOE's New Procedure for Approving LNG Export Permits: A More Sensible Approach," Brookings Institution, June 2014.

[9] David L. Goldwyn, "Refreshing European Energy Security Policy: How the U.S. Can Help," Brookings Institution, March 2014.

[10] Conglin Xu, "Global Oil Market Well Supplied Despite Disruptions to Producers," Oil and Gas Journal, July 47 2014.

[11] David L. Goldwyn and Cory R. Gill, ''Uncertain Energy: The Caribbean's Gamble with Venezuela,'' Brookings Institution, July 2014.
[12] Jed Bailey, Nils Janson, and Ramon Espinasa, Pre-Feasibility Study of the Potential Market for Natural Gas as a Fuel for Power Generation in the Caribbean, Inter-American Development Bank, December 2013.
[13] EIA Electric Power Monthly, June 23, 2014.

Senator MARKEY. Thank you, Mr. Goldwyn.

Next we are going to hear from Mr. Michael Breen, who is the executive director of the Truman National Security Project & Center for National Policy. Welcome, sir.

STATEMENT OF MICHAEL BREEN, EXECUTIVE DIRECTOR, TRUMAN NATIONAL SECURITY PROJECT & CENTER FOR NATIONAL POLICY, WASHINGTON, DC

Mr. BREEN. Thank you, Mr. Chairman, Chairman Markey, Ranking Member Barrasso. Thank you for the opportunity to testify today.

Although we find ourselves in a considerably better position with regard to energy than that of several years ago, the lack of diversified energy sources around the world continues to create vulnerabilities for the United States and our allies and opportunities for many of our rivals and adversaries.

Unfolding events in Iraq exemplify the ways in which energy and security are intertwined. Iraq is where I personally first came to understand energy security as a young Army officer fighting to defend fuel convoys against insurgent attack. A decade later, those same desert roads are once again a combat zone, with fuel supplies once again at the center of the fight. As is the case in other conflicts, nonstate actors in Iraq seek to capture and exploit energy resources as a source of funding.

One of ISIL's primary objectives during its recent offensive was the refinery at Baiji, which is the largest in Iraq. Reporting indicates that ISIL is raising as much as a million dollars a day from selling crude oil from fields it controls which is smuggled through Turkey and Iran. Revenues are then directed to purchase weapons, pay insurgent fighters, and help buy the loyalties of local tribal leaders and government officials.

Meanwhile, continued conflict in Iraq has a destabilizing effect on the global market. Dramatic increases in Iraq's oil production are an essential element in most projections of global supply growth. In IEA's World Energy Outlook, for example, the most likely scenario projects that Iraq will double its oil production by 2035. But that projected progress is currently at risk.

In the short term, some estimate that the loss of just a third of Iraqi oil production would cause a $37 a barrel rise in the price of oil. Longer term, though, investments in the Middle East may fall short of projections if regional conflict persists, which could lead to a potential supply shortfall into the 2020s.

Conflict in Ukraine also illustrates the increasingly dangerous use of energy as a geopolitical weapon, in this case with respect to natural gas. Russia has repeatedly used Ukraine's energy dependence and lack of diversification as leverage, cutting off natural gas exports. Meanwhile, about 16 percent of Europe's total natural gas consumption comes from Russia through Ukraine. Russia's manipulations of Ukraine's energy markets have created concerns about natural gas shortages in the European Union. Up to this point, EU sanctions against Russia and other responses to aggression in Crimea have fallen well short of United States action.

Despite dramatic advances in extractive technology, the geopolitical dynamics of energy are unlikely to move in America's favor beyond the short term, especially with regard to oil. Fundamentally, this is because demand in the developing world is projected to increase dramatically, offsetting increases in U.S. production. Oil demand is projected to grow to about 109 million barrels a day by 2035, with China becoming the world's largest consumer by about 2030.

Meanwhile, IEA projects that U.S. tight oil production will plateau in the 2020s before dropping to 9.2 million barrels a day by 2035, leaving us in roughly the same geopolitical position we were in before the shale revolution.

In addition, climate change makes our current energy system unsustainable, creating cascading risks and impacts around the globe.

Given these dynamics, a singular focus on fossil fuels production and export simply plays into the strengths of our competitors, while leaving the United States and our allies with continued long-term vulnerabilities. Ukraine again provides an excellent example. Many advocate United States LNG exports as a path to reducing Russian leverage. Such a policy has limited but clear benefits. However, LNG exports probably will not begin in substantial volume until 2017 at the earliest and reaching Ukraine will be difficult.

Meanwhile, Ukraine is so reliant on Russian natural gas in large part because it is the second-least efficient nation in Europe. If Ukraine were simply as energy efficiency as the average European country, it would reduce its natural gas consumption by more than 50 percent. That is why, as proposed by Chairman Markey earlier this year, the U.S. Government should leverage its full resources in assisting Ukraine to improve its energy efficiency, increase its domestic production, and reform its energy markets.

This approach applies more broadly as well. The United States should place greater emphasis on encouraging efficiency along with the development of renewable sources and more resilient distributed energy systems. The Department of Defense has been a clear leader in this respect, prioritizing critical investments in more diverse, resilient, and reliable energy sources in order to maximize freedom of action and minimize risk. The rest of government, along with the Nation as a whole, would do well to follow a similar approach.

Thank you.

[The prepared statement of Mr. Breen follows:]

PREPARED STATEMENT OF MICHAEL BREEN

Chairman Markey, Ranking Member Barrasso, distinguished members of the committee, thank you for the opportunity to testify today on the relationships between American foreign policy, energy policy, and climate change. I will focus my remarks today on the linkage between energy issues and America's most pressing geopolitical challenges.

The United States finds itself in a considerably better position with regard to energy than several years ago. Natural gas production in particular has expanded dramatically, putting the U.S. in a position to become a net exporter within the next several years. This is a positive development to be sure, and provides both strategic and economic opportunities. Energy continues to play a central role in many flashpoints around the world, however, including as a driver of armed conflict. While advances in technology have improved America's energy posture in the short term, many of our long-standing vulnerabilities persist and are likely to worsen in the longer term.

LACK OF ENERGY DIVERSITY CREATES SECURITY RISK

The lack of diversified energy sources around the world continues to create undue risk to American national security, the security of our key allies, and global stability and prosperity. In geopolitical terms, this lack of diversification creates vulnerabilities for the U.S. and our allies, and opportunities for many of our rivals and adversaries.

This dynamic is especially pronounced with regard to petroleum, since most major economies are overwhelmingly reliant on oil as a transportation fuel. The United States relies on oil for more than 93 percent of our transportation sector, and most advanced economies are in a roughly similar position. Given that oil is a globally traded fungible commodity, this single-source dependence on oil as a transportation fuel exposes the U.S. and our allies to the full range of risk associated with a complex and frequently manipulated global petroleum supply system. In other words, security and oil are deeply intertwined, with largely negative effects.

Iraq

Unfolding events in Iraq exemplify the ways in which energy and security are intertwined at every level of conflict. Iraq is where I first came to understand the security implications of energy dependence, as a young Army officer fighting to defend fuel convoys against insurgent attack. A decade later, those same desert roads outside of Baghdad are once again a combat zone, with fuel supplies still at the center of the fight.

As is the case in other conflicts, nonstate actors in Iraq exploit energy resources as a source of funding. Reporting indicates that ISIL is raising as much as $1 million a day from selling crude oil from oil fields in territory it controls, which is then smuggled into Turkey and Iran. In Syria, the Assad government is reportedly supplementing oil from Iran by purchasing oil from ISIL insurgents, even as its military fights them. Revenues are then directed to purchase weapons, pay insurgent fighters, and help buy the loyalties of local tribal leaders and government officials.

Oil resources and infrastructure are therefore key strategic points on the battlefield, shaping the course of the conflict at the tactical and operational levels of war. In one well-known example, one of ISIL's primary objectives during its recent offensive in Iraq was the refinery in Baiji, the largest in Iraq. Meanwhile, Kurdish military action in the conflict to date has been almost entirely defensive, with the sole exception of an early push to secure oil fields. KRG's seizure of Kirkuk oil province, in part intended to establish defense in depth for Kurdish areas, will also give the Kurds even greater financial and political autonomy from Baghdad.

This points to a third way in which access to oil supplies drives and shapes the ongoing conflict in Iraq. Regional instability and conflict within and between states across the MENA region is driven, in part, because of the uneven distribution of energy resources. This is certainly true in Iraq. Nearly 75 percent of Iraqi oil production is focused in the Shia-majority south, and the main export terminal in Basra is located there as well. Baghdad's failure to redistribute revenue from that oil production evenly across Iraq has been a major driver of sectarian and regional conflict.

Prized oil fields in the south currently remain productive, but are vulnerable to insurgent attacks and remain an important military prize for all parties to the conflict. Companies will most likely evacuate workers, and quickly, if there are serious security concerns in Basra. In the current climate, this continues to be a real possibility.

This is critical, because continued conflict in Iraq has a significant destabilizing effect on the deeply interdependent global oil market. This instability is already leading to economic and geopolitical consequences around the world, and could impact our economic recovery here at home given sufficient time. Dramatic increases in Iraq's oil production are an essential element in most projections of global supply growth. In IEA's World Energy Outlook, for example, the most likely scenario projects Iraq to double its oil production to 6.1mb/d by 2020, and 8.3 mb/d by 2035. According to IEA projections, Iraq makes up nearly 45 percent of anticipated global supply growth over the next decade.

All of that projected progress is currently at risk. In the short term, some estimate that the loss of just a third of Iraqi oil production would cause a \$37 a barrel rise in the price of oil. Saudi Arabia, home to nearly the entire world's spare capacity, is already stretched due to unanticipated short-term global demand growth. Longer term dynamics, while more difficult to predict, are potentially even more disturbing. Investments in the Middle East may fall short of projections if armed conflict and cascading instability across the region persist, leading to a potential supply shortfall in the 2020s.

Ukraine

Conflict in the Ukraine also illustrates the increasingly dangerous use of energy as a geopolitical weapon, in this case with respect to natural gas. Russia has repeatedly used Ukraine's energy dependence as leverage to disrupt the Ukrainian economy and exacerbate political rifts in the country. In 2012, about 60 percent of Ukraine's natural gas consumption and nearly 75 percent of its liquid fuels were imported from Russia. As tensions smoldered in Crimea and Eastern Ukraine this spring, Russia did not hesitate to capitalize on its dominant energy position for geopolitical ends, renouncing agreements establishing a natural gas energy giant, Gazprom.

Even as Russia has used energy dependence as a sword against Ukraine, it has employed similar dynamics as a shield against Western European interference in the conflict. Sixteen percent of Europe's total natural gas consumption comes from Russia through Ukraine. Russia's manipulations of Ukraine's energy markets have created concerns about natural gas shortages in the European Union. Up to this point, EU sanctions against Russia and other responses to aggression in Crimea have fallen well short of U.S. action. Instead, as proposed by Chairman Markey earlier this year, the U.S. government should leverage its full resources in assisting Ukraine to improve its energy efficiency, increase its domestic production, and reform its energy markets.

Northeast Asia

Despite rising tensions between Japan and China over possession of offshore islands and the continuing threat posed by North Korea, the security situation in the North China Sea region is not currently as dire as that in the Middle East and Eastern Europe. However, ongoing dynamics with respect to energy have a negative impact on U.S. interests and allies' security there as well. Earlier this year, Russia and China signed a 30-year gas supply agreement worth approximately \$400 billion. This agreement may draw the two great powers into deeper alignment, with negative repercussions for the U.S. and our allies.

Meanwhile, Japan's energy situation continues to evolve amid considerable uncertainty. More than a quarter (26 percent) of Japan's electricity came from nuclear power plants before the Fukushima disaster. Now, with all of its nuclear plants on indefinite suspension, Japan is the world's leading importer of liquefied natural gas. Japan alone consumed over a third (37 percent) of global LNG in 2012. In an effort to meet this need, Japan is reportedly considering a natural gas pipeline to Russia to bring in LNG from Siberia. While this would have some benefits for Japan, Russia's demonstrated willingness to use energy supplies for coercion should give us pause.

FUTURE TRENDS

Despite dramatic advances in extractive technology, the geopolitical dynamics of energy are unlikely to move in America's favor beyond the short term, especially with regard to oil. Fundamentally, this is because demand in the developing world is projected to increase dramatically, offsetting increases in U.S. production. Oil demand is projected to grow by 19 mb/d to 109 mb/d by 2035. Virtually all of this increased demand is expected to come from non-OECD countries. China is projected to become the world's largest consumer in 2029, growing to 18mb/d by 2035, while demand from India and the Middle East will likely grow even more rapidly than China's.

Meanwhile, IEA projects that U.S. tight oil production will reach a plateau in the 2020s, before dropping to 9.2 mb/d by 2035 mb/d by 2035—leaving us in much the same position we were in before the shale revolution. The global market is projected to remain fairly tight overall along the way, meaning price volatility will continue to be a problem over the next several decades. This places the U.S. and our allies at risk of continued overreliance on the same large-scale holders of conventional resources who energy system unsustainable, creating cascading risks and impacts around the globe and across the full range of human activity.

Given these dynamics, a singular focus on fossil fuels production and export simply plays into the strengths of our competitors while leaving the U.S. and our allies with continued vulnerabilities. The U.S. should also encourage investments in renewable energy and energy efficiency through technology sharing and targeted loans.

Ukraine provides an excellent example. Many advocate U.S. LNG exports as a path to reducing Russian leverage. Such a policy has limited but clear benefits, and should be pursued. However, LNG exports probably won't begin at substantial volume until 2017 at the earliest, and reaching Ukraine will be difficult. Turkey in particular is likely to resist allowing LNG tankers through the Bosphorus, due to safety, environmental, and economic concerns.

Meanwhile, Ukraine is so reliant on Russian natural gas in large part because it is the second most energy inefficient nation in Europe, with energy subsidies making up nearly 8 percent of GDP. If Ukraine were simply as energy efficient as the average European country, it would reduce its natural gas consumption by more than 50 percent. The U.S. should seize the opportunity to improve Ukraine's position by prioritizing investments in energy efficiency. We should also tap existing U.S. and international expertise to increase and diversify Ukraine's domestic energy production, including renewables.

This approach applies more broadly as well. The U.S. should place greater emphasis on encouraging efficiency, along with the development of renewable sources and more resilient distributed energy systems. The Department of Defense has been a clear leader in this respect, teaming with partner nations to improve fuel efficiency and reduce energy demand across our combined forces. At the same time, DOD has prioritized critical investments in more diverse, resilient, and reliable energy sources in order to maximize freedom of action and minimize risk. The rest of government, along with the nation as a whole, would do well to follow a similar approach.

Senator MARKEY. Thank you, Mr. Breen.

Our final witness, Ms. Mary Hutzler, is distinguished senior fellow for the Institute of Energy Research. We welcome you.

STATEMENT OF MARY HUTZLER, DISTINGUISHED SENIOR FELLOW, INSTITUTE FOR ENERGY RESEARCH, BERLIN, MD

Ms. HUTZLER. Chairman Markey, Dr. Barrasso, and members of the committee, thank you for the invitation to testify today concerning the prospect of greater energy security and particularly how the contours of various climate policies are shaping our own domestic energy future and that of our allies.

I want to begin by congratulating you, Chairman Markey, for your successful bid to fill the seat vacated by Secretary of State John Kerry. I have had many opportunities through the years to testify before you during your nearly four decades of service in the House of Representatives and I welcome the opportunity to continue that dialogue.

For more than 7 years I have served IER and before that I held several management positions at the Energy Information Administration, including as Acting Administrator. In all that time, neither energy analysts at EIA nor policymakers in the U.S. Congress were able to predict the transformation of America's domestic energy frontier that occurred over the last few years. For decades, U.S. energy policy had been guided by the ever-elusive quest for diminishing energy resources. Our allies around the world also felt the squeeze of perceived energy scarcity. Meanwhile, climate alarm intensified a political push for renewable energy.

Data now exists to examine the effects of these policies, both on the climate and on the economies of the nations who adopted aggressive agendas for decarbonization. Over the course of the last decade, countries across the European Union have pursued the specter of a green energy future with unparalleled enthusiasm. Through various tax measures, taxpayer-funded subsidies, mandates, surcharges, and feed-in tariffs, our allies across the Atlantic have provided us an instructive lesson.

Today industrial electricity prices in the EU are two to five times higher than in the United States. According to the European Commission, electricity prices in Europe have risen 37 percent more than those in the United States when indexed against 2005 prices. By 2020, as many as 1.4 million additional European households are expected to be in what some analysts refer to as "energy poverty."

The EU system of cap and trade, a variation of which narrowly passed the U.S. House of Representatives in June 2009 but never became law, has proven fertile terrain for fraudsters, tax cheats, market manipulators, and various cyber criminals who exploit the inherent weaknesses of carbon trading schemes. According to the market analysts at Bloomberg, as much as 7 percent of the total carbon market is based on fraudulent trading in a given year.

Additionally, some of our European allies are now facing the steep decline of their economies and a dramatic rise in their unemployment rolls as they struggle under a heavy green energy burden. In Spain, for each megawatt of wind energy installed more than four jobs were lost. For each megawatt of solar, nearly 13 jobs were lost. And in the past 7 years, Spain's unemployment rate has jumped from 9 percent to more than 25 percent. Fortunately, Spain's policymakers are trying to stop the hemorrhage that their quest for green energy has exasperated.

Wind and solar cannot sustain a growing, vibrant economy. These technologies do not create long-term jobs and they cannot supply reliable electricity when consumers need it most. In Germany, where utilities have been ordered to generate 50 percent of their electricity from renewable sources by 2030, the EU's largest economy is now risking what their own energy minister called "de-industrialization." Germany's green energy agenda, phase-out of its nuclear units, and restrictions on development of its domestic resources have resulted in high electricity prices, dependence on Russia for natural gas supplies, and increased greenhouse gas emissions.

In the U.K., nearly one-fifth of the nation's population is now in energy poverty, up from 6 percent just a decade ago. In Australia, where a short-lived carbon tax threatened to set the world's 12th-largest economy back decades, the government has repealed it to mitigate the harm caused by a tax that neither helped the environment nor the economy.

The policies of these countries have followed a similar pattern. The government passes ambitious green energy laws, electricity rates rise as subsidies increase out of control, job losses pile up, and the government is forced to consider amending or repealing its misguided policies.

Europe's green energy policies have contributed to its economic slowdown, where Europe is now unable to meet its minimal NATO commitments to fund defense. And because Russia is an important energy supplier, Europe is increasingly reluctant to act against aggression.

The United States must not follow a similar course. The bright horizon of America's domestic energy future is not guaranteed and policymakers should temper their enthusiasm for renewables with the real world facts, now observed with undeniable effects for those who have pursued the green energy dream.

Thank you for the opportunity to testify. I am happy to answer any questions.

[The prepared statement of Ms. Hutzler follows:]

PREPARED STATEMENT OF MARY J. HUTZLER

The Institute for Energy Research (IER) is a nonprofit organization that conducts research and evaluates public policies in energy markets. IER articulates free market positions that respect private property rights and promote efficient outcomes for energy consumers and producers. IER staff and scholars educate policymakers and the general public on the economic and environmental benefits of free market energy. The organization was founded in 1989 as a public foundation under Section 501(c)(3) of the Internal Revenue Code. Funding for the institute comes from tax-deductible contributions of individuals, foundations, and corporations.

Thank you for the opportunity to supply this testimony for the committee's use.

The United States is in the midst of a domestic energy renaissance that has lowered our import dependency and increased our security. However, there are many policymakers that seek to restrict the availability of our natural resources and make energy less affordable for Americans. Lessons can be learned from many of our allies that have tried carbon restriction policies and have had poor results.

Europe, for example, has pursued some of the most aggressive "green" energy policies in the world. Countries across the European Union have passed laws to promote renewable energy technologies, curb greenhouse gas (GHG) emissions, and decrease energy consumption. To achieve these goals, European governments have imposed various schemes, taxes, subsidies, and mandates, including cap and trade, feed-in tariffs and surcharges that force consumers to foot the bill for expensive green energy technologies.

Carbon restriction and other "green" policies have slowed the economies of these allies, moved industries offshore, made jobs more difficult to obtain, and lowered the income power of their citizens. While each country has had a somewhat unique experience, all follow a similar pattern: the government passes ambitious green energy laws; electricity prices rise as subsidies increase; and then the government considers amending or repealing its misguided policies.

Australia, for example, having imposed a carbon tax, has now approved legislation to remove it. And, other countries that have subsidized renewable energy are slashing those subsidies due to the impact on their economies, electricity rates, and energy poverty levels. This testimony will highlight carbon restriction policies in the European Union (EU) and Australia and their resulting impact.

EUROPEAN UNION EMISSIONS TRADING SCHEME

The Emissions Trading Scheme (ETS) was launched by the EU in January 2005 as an attempt to comply with the 1997 Kyoto Protocol. It was the world's first cross-border greenhouse gas emissions (GHG) trading program, regulating more than 11,500 installations and about 45 percent of total EU carbon dioxide emissions. Under the ETS, European companies must hold permits to allow them to emit carbon dioxide. A certain number of those permits were distributed at no cost to the industries that must reduce their output of carbon dioxide emissions. If businesses emit less carbon dioxide than the permits they hold, they can either keep the excess permits for future use or sell the excess permits and make a profit on them.

The early results of the program were that EU emissions were not significantly lowered until the global recession hit in 2008, which lowered emissions for all countries. There were also misuses and abuses in the system because of its complexity, politicized decisionmaking, and the incentive to manipulate it.

Before the global recession hit, some EU countries saw faster carbon dioxide emissions growth than the United States which was not subject to the policy. From 2000 to 2006, the rate of growth of European emissions under the cap-and-trade policy was almost 5 times higher than the rate of growth in emissions in the United States.[1] After the global recession, however, EU carbon dioxide emissions in 2009 were almost 8 percent below 2008 levels.[2] Due to the global recession, carbon dioxide emissions, in many cases, were lowered below the targets set by the cap-and-trade policy, so companies did not have to take further actions to reduce their emissions.[3] Severe downturns in economic activity result in significant reductions in emissions. Because the free allocation of permits was based on future estimates of higher emissions levels, which did not materialize, there were too many free government-issued permits. As a result, companies hit hard by the recession were able to make profits by selling the excess permits but chose not to pass those savings onto their customers. Consumers ended up paying higher energy and commodity costs; taxpayers paid for the program's implementation; and a new middleman was created to run the carbon permit trading program.[4]

Europe found the costs of the program to be large. In 2006, individual business and sectors had to pay ÷24.9 billion for permits totaling over 1 billion tons. In 2011, the global carbon markets were valued at US$176 billion, with 10.3 billion carbon credits traded.[5] The World Watch Institute estimated the costs of running a trading system designed to meet the EU's Kyoto obligations at about $5 billion. The costs of a trading system to meet the EU's commitments of a 20-percent reduction by 2020 (against a 1990 baseline) were estimated to be about $80 billion annually.[6]

Unlike traditional commodities, which at some time during the course of their market exchange must be physically delivered to someone, carbon credits do not represent a physical commodity, which makes them particularly vulnerable to fraud and other illegal activity. Carbon markets, like other financial markets, are at risk of exploitation by criminals due to the large amount of money invested, the immaturity of the regulations and lack of oversight and transparency. The illegal activities identified include[7]:

- Fraudulent manipulation of measurements to claim more carbon credits from a project than were actually obtained;
- Sale of carbon credits that either do not exist or belong to someone else;
- False or misleading claims with respect to the environmental or financial benefits of carbon market investments;
- Exploitation of weak regulations in the carbon market to commit financial crimes, such as money laundering, securities fraud or tax fraud; and
- Computer hacking/ phishing to steal carbon credits and theft of personal information.

German prosecutors, for example, searched 230 offices and homes of Deutsche Bank, Germany's largest bank, and RWE, Germany's second-biggest utility, to investigate 180 million euros ($238 million U.S.) of tax evasion linked to emissions trading. The U.K., France, and the Netherlands also investigated carbon traders, who committed fraud by collecting the tax, and disappearing without returning the tax funds. According to estimates from Bloomberg New Energy Finance, about 400 million metric tons of emission trades may have been fraudulent in 2009, or about 7 percent of the total market.[8] Tax evasion linked to emissions trading is still a problem. This year, for example, Frankfurt prosecutors sought the arrest of a British national in connection with suspected tax fraud worth 58 million euros ($80 million).[9]

Another problem is with the lack of predictability regarding the emissions permit price. Companies need to know the price for long-term planning to decide on what actions they should take. The EU permit price ranged by a factor of 3, but even at the higher price range, it was insufficient to meet the emission reduction targets before the global recession hit.[10] A cap-and-trade policy is a highly complex system to implement because there are a large number of participants and the components of the system are difficult to get right as EU's experience has shown.

Last year, the EU commenced phase three of the ETS toward meeting their target of a 40-percent reduction in greenhouse gas emissions below 1990 levels by 2030.[11] Phase 3, which has a number of significant rule changes, will continue until 2020. As of 2011, carbon dioxide emissions of the original 27 member EU were just 8 percent below 1990 levels, and the majority of the reduction was achieved by the global recession. That means the EU has a long way to go to meet its target. In the meantime, energy prices have increased and more and more Europeans are facing fuel poverty, meaning they pay more than 10 percent of their household income for energy.

For example, industrial electricity prices are two to five times higher in the EU than in the United States and are expected to increase more.

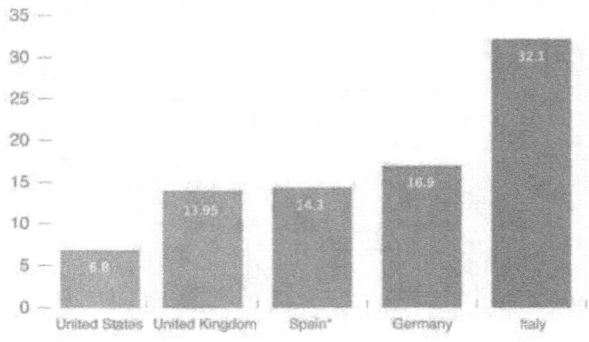

Source: International Industrial Electricity Prices, https://www.gov.uk/government/statistical-data-sets/international-industrial-energy-prices

Europe's once comfortable middle class is being pushed into energy poverty as a result of the carbon reduction measures and EU's renewable programs (discussed later). According to the European Commission, electricity prices in the Organization for Economic Cooperation (OECD) Europe have risen 37 percent more than those in the United States when indexed against 2005 prices. By 2020, at least 1.4 million additional European households are expected to be in energy poverty.

EU's ETS and clean energy programs have not significantly reduced emissions, but rather have dramatically raised energy prices, increased national debt, driven businesses out of Europe, led to massive job losses and unemployment, greatly increased energy poverty, and have been plagued by fraud and corruption. This economic malaise, in turn, has made Europe less capable of expending funds for their national defense needs and has contributed to the weakening of multilateral defense organizations like NATO. The European members of NATO are now spending less than 2 percent of their GDP on defense spending, which is below NATO guidance.[12]

AUSTRALIA'S CARBON TAX

Australia implemented a carbon tax in 2012. Below is a schematic of Australia's plans, beginning in 2009, for a cap-and-trade program and carbon tax. The carbon tax, which is currently set at $24.15 Australian currency ($22.70 U.S.) per metric ton, was initially implemented in July 2012 and was designed as a precursor to a cap and trade scheme, with the transition to a flexible carbon price as part of the trading program beginning in 2015. The tax applies directly to around 370 Australian businesses. But the September 7, 2013, election put a damper on the program.

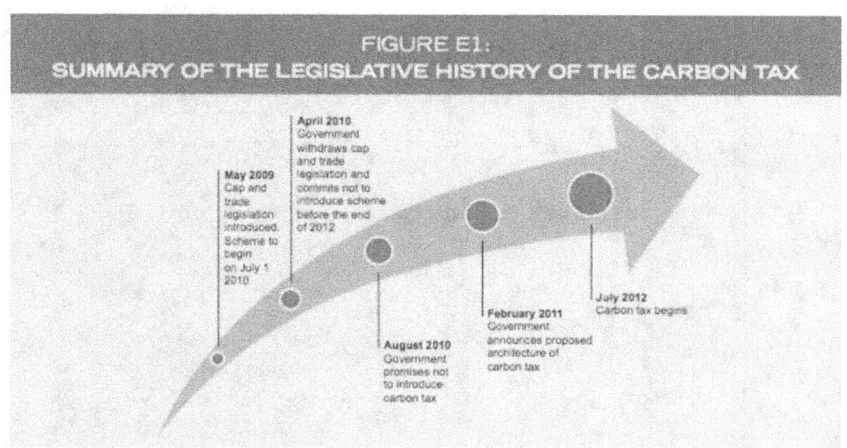

FIGURE E1:
SUMMARY OF THE LEGISLATIVE HISTORY OF THE CARBON TAX

Source: *Australia's Carbon Tax: An Economic Evaluation, September 2013, http://instituteforenergyresearch.org/wp-content/uploads/2013/09/IER_AustraliaCarbonTaxStudy.pdf*

Australia's new government wants to dismantle the legislation that levies fees on carbon emissions and replace it with taxpayer funded grants to companies and projects that reduce emissions. The Emissions Reduction Fund would be funded at A$2.55 billion ($2.4 billion U.S.).[13] Repealing Australia's carbon tax on July 1, 2014, is estimated to [14]:

- Reduce the cost of living of its citizens—the Australian Treasury estimates that removing the carbon tax in 2014 to 2015 will reduce the average costs of living across all households by about $550 more than they would otherwise be in 2014 to 2015.
- Lower the cost of retail electricity by around 9 percent and retail gas prices by around 7 percent than they would otherwise be in 2014 to 2015.
- Boost Australia's economic growth, increase jobs and enhance Australia's international competitiveness by removing an unnecessary tax, which hurts businesses and families.
- Reduce annual ongoing compliance costs for around 370 entities by almost $90 million per annum.
- Remove over 1,000 pages of primary and subordinate legislation.

Australia's lower House of Parliament voted to scrap the carbon tax on July 14, and the Australian Senate voted in favor on July 17, 2014.[15] According to Tony Abbott, Australian Prime Minister speaking at a news conference, "Today the tax that you voted to get rid of is finally gone, a useless destructive tax which damaged jobs, which hurt families' cost of living and which didn't actually help the environment is finally gone." The repeal will save Australian voters and business around A$9 billion ($8.4 billion U.S.) a year.[16]

Australia's residents found the carbon tax experience to include soaring electricity prices, rising unemployment, income tax hikes, and additional command-and-control regulations. Electricity prices increased 15 percent over the course of a year (which included the highest quarterly increase on record), and companies laid off workers because of the tax.

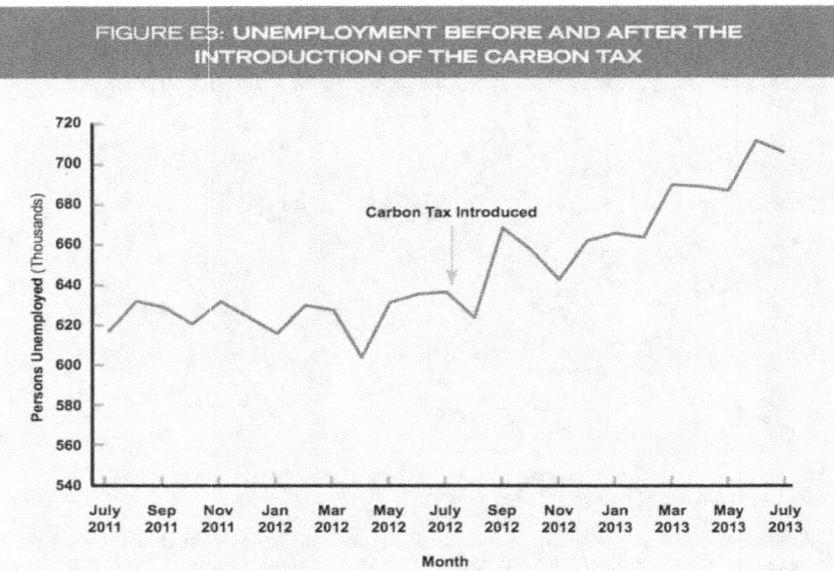

FIGURE E3: UNEMPLOYMENT BEFORE AND AFTER THE INTRODUCTION OF THE CARBON TAX

Source: Australia's Carbon Tax: An Economic Evaluation, September 2013, http://instituteforenergyresearch.org/wp-content/uploads/2013/09/IER_AustraliaCarbonTaxStudy.pdf

Further, government data shows that the tax had not reduced the level of Australia's domestically produced carbon dioxide emissions, which is not surprising, since under the carbon tax Australia's domestic emissions were not expected to fall below current levels until 2045.[17]

RENEWABLE SUBSIDIES IN EUROPE

As part of Europe's effort to reduce greenhouse gas emissions to comply with the Kyoto Protocol, EU set mandates for renewable generation (20 percent of its electricity to be generated by renewable energy by 2020) coupled with hefty renewable subsidies as enticements. The Europeans have found that these subsidies have grown too large, are hurting their economies, and as a result, they are now slashing the subsidies. In fact, the costs have become so enormous that governments in European countries are unilaterally rewriting their contracts with renewable generating firms and reneging on the generous deals they initially provided. Spain, for example, ended its feed-in tariff, which guaranteed an extremely high price for renewable power, replacing it with either a much lower subsidy or no subsidy, depending on the circumstance.

Spain

In order to enhance renewable energy sources in Spain, the Government enacted legislation to reach 20 percent of electric production from qualified renewable energy by 2010. To meet this target, the government found it needed to provide incentives to ensure the market penetration of renewable energy, including providing above-market rates for renewable-generated electricity and requiring that electric utility companies purchase all renewable energy produced.

In 1994, Spain implemented feed-in tariffs to jump start its renewable industry by providing long-term contracts that pay the owners of renewable projects above-market rates for the electricity produced.[18] Because renewable technologies generally cost more than conventional fossil fuel technologies, the government guaranteed that renewable firms would get a higher cost for their technologies. But, because the true costs of renewable energy were never passed on to the consumers of electricity in Spain, the government needed to find a way to make renewable power payments and electricity revenues meet.

Since 2000, Spain provided renewable producers $41 billion more for their power than it received from its consumers.[19] (For reference, Spain's economy is about one-twelfth the size of the U.S. economy.) In 2012, the discrepancy between utility payments to renewable power producers and the revenue they collected from customers was 5.6 billion euros ($7.3 billion), despite the introduction of a 7-percent tax on generation.[20] The 2012 gap represented a 46-percent increase over the previous year's shortfall.

This massive rate deficit should not come as a surprise. For 5 years, IER has warned of this problem beginning when Dr. Gabriel Calzada released his paper on the situation in Spain and testified before Congress.[21] He found that Spain's ''green jobs'' agenda resulted in job losses elsewhere in the country's economy. For each ''green'' megawatt installed, 5.28 jobs on average were lost in the Spanish economy; for each megawatt of wind energy installed, 4.27 jobs were lost; and for each megawatt of solar installed, 12.7 jobs were lost. Although solar energy may appear to employ many workers in the plant's construction, in reality it consumes a large amount of capital that would have created many more jobs in other parts of the economy. The study also found that 9 out of 10 jobs in the renewable industry were temporary.[22, 23]

Spain's unemployment rate has more than doubled between 2008 and 2013. In January 2013, Spain's unemployment rate was 26 percent, the highest among EU member states.[24] Spain's youth unemployment (under the age of 25) reached 57.7 percent in November 2013, surpassing Greece's youth unemployment rate of 54.8 percent in September 2013.[25]

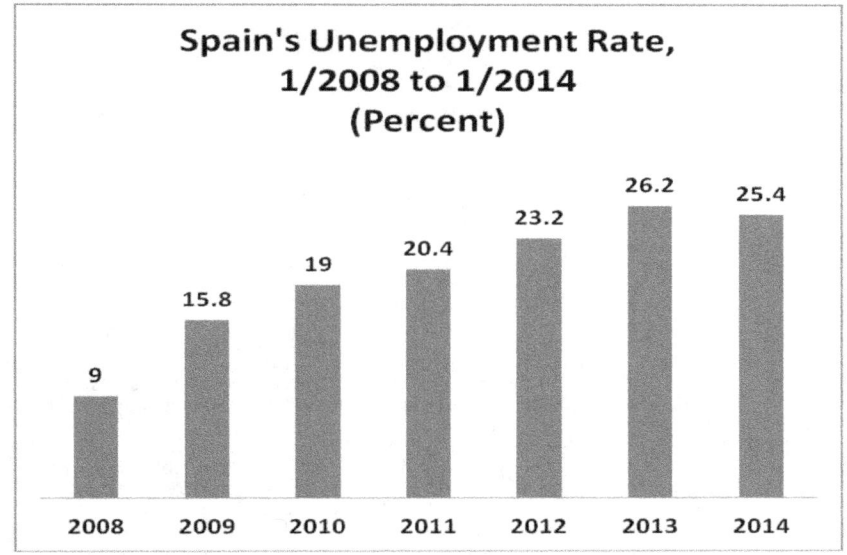

Source: Eurostat

The Spanish Government did not believe Dr. Calzada 5 years ago, but they have now been hit in the face with reality. To recover the lost revenues from the extravagant subsidies, the Spanish Government ended its feed-in tariff program for renewables, which paid the renewable owners an extremely high guaranteed price for their power as can be seen by the deficit. Currently, renewable power in Spain gets the market price plus a subsidy which the country deems more ''reasonable.'' Companies' profits are capped at a 7.4-percent return, after which renewable owners must sell their power at market rates. The measure is retroactive to when the renewable plant was first built.[26] Therefore, some renewable plants, if they have already received the 7.4 percent return, are receiving only the market price for their electricity.

Further, wind projects built before 2005 will no longer receive any form of subsidy, which affects more than a third of Spain's wind projects. As a consequence of the government's actions to rein in their subsidies and supports, Spain's wind sector is estimated to have laid off 20,000 workers.

The Spanish Government also slashed subsidies to solar power, subsidizing just 500 megawatts of new solar projects, down from 2,400 megawatts in 2008.[27] Its solar sector, which once employed 60,000 workers, now employs just 5,000. In 2013, solar investment in Spain dropped by 90 percent from its 2011 level of $10 billion.

Spain's 20 percent renewable energy share of generation from wind and solar power has come at a very high cost to the nation.

SPAIN NET GENERATION SHARES BY FUEL TYPE, 2012

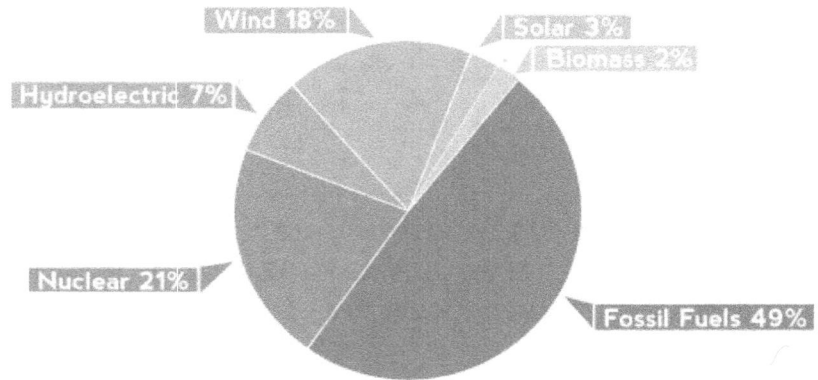

Source: Energy Information Administration, International Data Base

IER

Germany

In Germany, as part of the country's "Energiewende," or "energy transformation," electric utilities have been ordered to generate 35 percent of their electricity from renewable sources by 2020, 50 percent by 2030, 65 percent by 2040, and 80 percent by 2050. To encourage production of renewable energy, the German government instituted a feed-in tariff early, even before Spain.

In 1991, Germany established the Electricity Feed-in Act, which mandated that renewables "have priority on the grid and that investors in renewables must receive sufficient compensation to provide a return on their investment irrespective of electricity prices on the power exchange." [28] In other words, utilities are required to purchase electricity from renewable sources they may not want or need at above-market rates. For example, solar photovoltaics had a feed-in tariff of 43 euro cents per kilowatt hour ($0.59 U.S. per kilowatt hour), over 8 times the wholesale price of electricity and over four times the feed-in tariff for onshore wind power. A subsequent law passed in 2000, the Renewable Energy Act (EEG), extended feed-in tariffs for 20 years.[29]

Originally, to allow for wind and solar generation technologies to mature into competitive industries, Germany planned to extend the operating lives of its existing nuclear fleet by an average of 12 years. But, the Fukushima nuclear accident in Japan caused by a tsunami changed Germany's plans and the country quickly shuttered eight nuclear reactors and is phasing out its other nine reactors by 2022, leaving the country's future electricity production mostly to renewable energy and coal.[30]

Coal consumption in Germany in 2012 was the highest it has been since 2008, and electricity from brown coal (lignite) in 2013 reached the highest level since 1990 when East Germany's Soviet-era coal plants began to be shut down. German electricity generation from coal increased to compensate for the loss of the hastily shuttered nuclear facilities. Germany is now building new coal capacity at a rapid rate, approving 10 new coal plants to come on line within the next 2 years to deal with expensive natural gas generation and the high costs and unreliability of renewable energy.[31] As a result, carbon dioxide emissions are increasing.

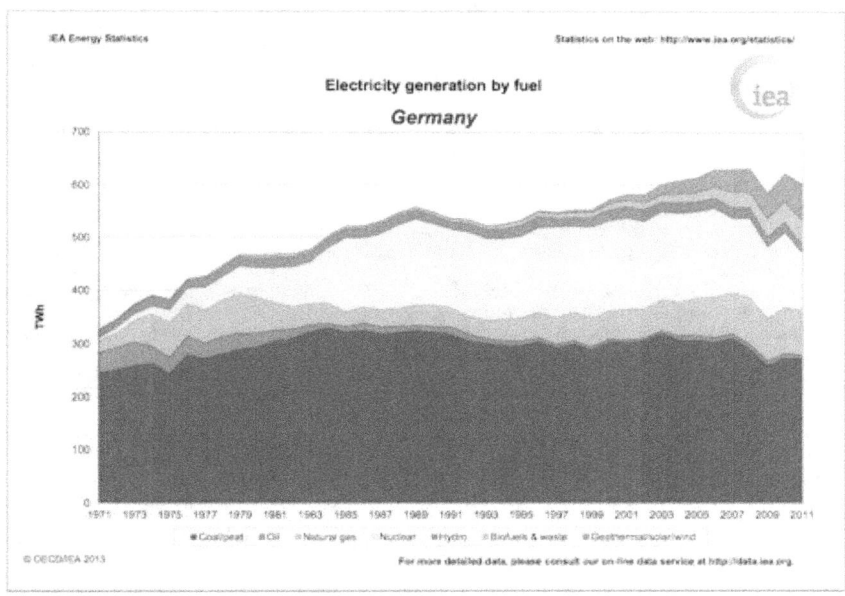

In 2013, Germany's carbon dioxide emissions increased by 2.4 percent over 2012 levels.[32]

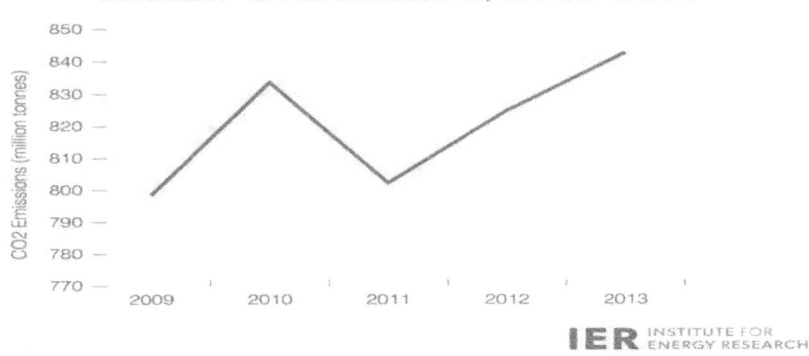

Source: BP, Statistical Review 2014 workbook, Statistical Review 2014, http://www.bp.com/en/global/corporate/about-bp/energy-economics/statistical-review-of-world-energy/statistical-review-downloads.html

While the United States is using low cost domestic natural gas to lower coal-fired generation, in Germany, the cost of natural gas is high since it is purchased at rates competitive with oil. Also, Germany is worried about its natural gas supplies since it gets a sizable amount from Russia. While domestic shale gas resources are an alternative, particularly since the Germans are hydraulic fracturing pioneers and have used the technology to extract tight gas since the 1960s, Germany's Environment Minister has proposed a prohibition on hydraulic fracturing until 2021 in response to opposition from the Green Party.[33] According to the Energy Information Administration, Germany has 17 trillion cubic feet of technically recoverable shale gas resources.[34]

Germany has some of the highest costs of electricity in Europe and its consumers are becoming energy poor. In 2012, the average price of electricity in Germany was 36.25 cents per kilowatt hour,[35] compared to just 11.88 cents for U.S. households, triple the U.S. average residential price.[36] These prices led Germany's Energy Minister to recently caution that they risk the "deindustrialization" of the economy.

In addition to high electricity prices, Germans are paying higher taxes to subsidize expensive green energy. The surcharge for Germany's Renewable Energy Levy that taxes households to subsidize renewable energy production increased by 50 percent between 2012 and 2013—from ÷3.6 cents (4.97 U.S. cents) to ÷5.28 cents (6.7 cents) per kilowatt hour, costing a German family of four about ÷250 ($324) per year, including sales tax.[37] The German Government raised the surcharge again at the start of this year by 18 percent to ÷6.24 cents per kilowatt hour (8.61 U.S. cents) representing about a fifth of residential utility bills,[38] making the total feed-in tariff support for 2014 equal to ÷21.5 billion ($29.6 billion).[39] As a result, 80 German utilities had to raise electricity rates by 4 percent, on average, in February, March, and April of this year.

The poor suffer disproportionately from higher energy costs because they spend a higher percentage of their income on energy. As many as 800,000 Germans have had their power cut off because of an inability to pay for rising energy costs, including 200,000 of Germany's long-term unemployed.[40]

Adding to this is a further disaster. Large offshore wind farms have been built in Germany's less populated north and the electricity must be transported to consumers in the south. But, 30 wind turbines off the North Sea island of Borkum are operating without being connected to the grid because the connection cable is not expected to be completed until sometime later this year. Further, the seafloor must be swept for abandoned World War II ordnance before a cable can be run to shore. The delay will add $27 million to the $608 million cost of the wind park. And, in order to keep the turbines from rusting, the turbines are being run with diesel.[41] [42]

Germany's power grid has been strained by new wind and solar projects both on and offshore, making the government invest up to $27 billion over the next decade to build about 1,700 miles of high-capacity power lines and to upgrade existing lines. The reality is that not only is renewable energy more expensive, but it also requires expensive transmission investments that existing sources do not, thus compounding the impact on consumers and businesses.

Germany knows reforms are necessary. On January 29, the German Cabinet backed a plan for new commercial and industrial renewable power generators to pay a charge on the electricity they consume. As part of the reform of the Renewable Energy Sources Act, the proposal would charge self generators 70 percent of the renewable subsidy surcharge, (i.e. the ÷6.24 cents per kilowatt hour). Under the proposal, the first 10 megawatt hours would be exempt for owners of solar photovoltaic projects that are less than 10 kilowatts. According to the German Solar Energy Industry Association, about 83 percent of solar self generators would be subject to the new charge. Another reform being considered is a reduction in the feed-in tariff from the current average of ÷17 cents (23.47 U.S. cents) per kilowatt hour to ÷12 cents (16.56 U.S. cents) per kilowatt hour.[43]

On July 11, Germany's upper House of Parliament passed changes to the Renewable Energy Sources Act, which will take effect as planned on August 1. The law lowers subsidies for new green power plants and spreads the power-price surcharge more equally among businesses.[44]

United Kingdom

Unlike Spain and Germany, the United Kingdom (U.K.) started its feed-in-tariff program to incentivize renewable energy relatively late, in 2010.[45] Hydroelectric, solar, and wind units all have specified tariffs that electric utilities must pay for their energy, which are above market rates. Like the other countries, the U.K. has a mandate for renewable energy. The United Kingdom is targeting a 15-percent share of energy generated from renewable sources in gross final energy consumption and a 31-percent share of electricity demand from electricity generated from renewable sources by 2020.[46] The U.K. generates about 12 percent of its electricity from renewable energy today. The increased renewable power will cost consumers 120 pounds a year (about $200) above their current average energy bill of 1,420 pounds ($2,362).[47]

The U.K. is closing coal-fired power plants to reduce carbon dioxide emissions in favor of renewable energy. In the U.K., 8,200 megawatts of coal-fired power plants have been shuttered, with an additional 13,000 megawatts at risk over the next 5 years, according to the Confederation of U.K. Coal Producers.[48] The U.K.'s energy regulator is worried that the amount of capacity over-peak demand this winter will be under 2 percent—a very low, scary amount for those charged with keeping the lights on—and the lowest in Western Europe.

Beginning in January 2016, the European Union will require electric utilities to add further emission reduction equipment to plants or close them by either 2023 or when they have run for 17,500 hours. Because the equipment is expensive, costing over 100 million pounds ($167 million) per gigawatt of capacity, only one U.K. electricity producer has chosen to install the required technology. Most of the existing coal-fired plants are expected to be shuttered since only one coal-fired power plant has been built in the U.K. since the early 1970s.

To deal with the reliability issue, the U.K. Government is hosting an auction for backup power, but it is unclear how it will work. According to the Department for Energy and Climate Change, electricity producers will be able to bid in an auction to take place this December to provide backup power for 2018. The program, called a capacity market, is expected to ensure sufficient capacity and security of supply. The Department estimates that the U.K. power industry needs around 110 billion pounds ($184 billion) of investment over the next 10 years.

The Renewable Energy Foundation (REF) estimates that consumers currently pay more than £1 billion ($1.66 billion) a year in subsidies to renewable energy producers—twice the wholesale cost of electricity. Those subsidies are expected to increase to £6 billion ($10 billion) a year by 2020 to meet a 30 percent target of providing electricity from renewable energy.[49] As a result, a growing number of U.K. households are in energy poverty. In 2003, roughly 6 percent of the United Kingdom's population was in energy poverty; a decade later, nearly one-fifth of the nation's population is in energy poverty.

PERCENT OF U.K. HOUSEHOLDS IN ENERGY POVERTY

Percent of UK Households in Energy Poverty

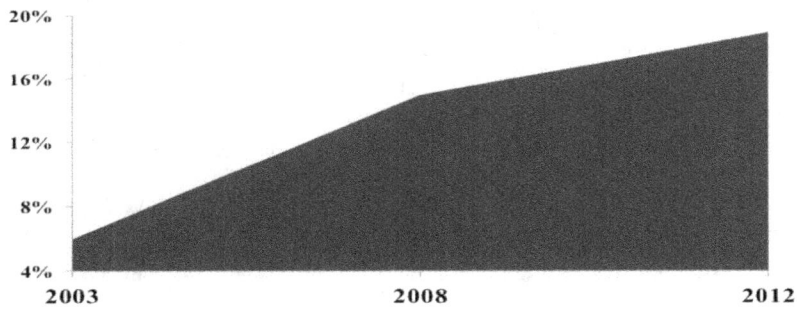

Source: The Failure of Global Carbon Policies, June 11, 2014, http://acclive.com/article/the-failure-of-global-carbon-policies.html

As a result, the government has proposed that renewable companies sell their electricity to the national grid under a competitive bidding system. The new proposal limits the total amount of subsidies available for green energy, which were previously effectively limitless. The reduction in subsidies has led to renewable developers scrapping plans amid claims that the proposal will make future renewable development unprofitable.[50]

The U.K. is both cutting the level of their feed-in tariffs and the length of time they are available. Effective July 1, 2013, the feed-in tariff for solar generated electricity was reduced from 15.44 pence (24 cents U.S.) to 14.90 pence per kilowatt hour. In October 2011, it was 43.3 pence (67.5 cents U.S.) per kilowatt hour—almost three times the reduced level.[51] Also, the length of time for the subsidy entitlement is being reduced—for example, it will be 15 years instead of 20 years for wind farms built after 2017. The reductions indicate that the original subsidies were overgenerous and that wind turbines are unlikely to have an economic life of 20 years.[52]

But, according to the Climate Change Committee (CCC), without tougher action, Britain will miss its 31 percent target of cutting emissions, managing only a 21-percent reduction instead, which will hinder meeting its commitment to cut greenhouse gas emissions by 80 percent of 1990 levels by 2050. The CCC called for more progress on insulating homes, promoting the uptake of ground source and air source heat pumps, and investment in support for electric vehicles. It also urged the U.K. to end the ''high degree of uncertainty'' about its support for renewable energy and provide funding for commercializing offshore wind.[53]

Italy

Similar to Germany and Spain, Italy also used feed-in tariffs to spur renewable development, and found it too costly. In 2005, Italy introduced its solar subsidy plan, providing solar power with premiums ranging from Euro 0.445 ($0.60 U.S.) per kilowatt hour to euro 0.490 ($0.66 U.S.) per kilowatt hour.[54] That subsidy resulted in the construction of more than 17,000 megawatts of solar capacity. In 2011, Italy's solar market was the world's largest, but that market has slowed due to the removal of subsidies.

Italy ceased granting feed-in tariffs for new installations after July 6, 2013, because its subsidy program had reached its budget cap—a limit of 6.7 billion euros ($8.9 billion) as of June 6, 2013. The law restricts above-market rates for solar energy a month after the threshold is reached. Without tariffs, the Italian solar market will need to depend on net metering (where consumers can sell the power they generate themselves to the grid) and income tax deductions for support.[55]

Italy also undertook other measures. In 2012, the government charged all solar producers a five-cent tax per kilowatt hour on all self-consumed energy. The government also curtailed purchasing power from solar self generators when their output exceeded the amount the system needed. Those provisions were followed in 2013 by the government instituting a ''Robin Hood tax'' of 10.5 percent to renewable energy producers with more than ÷3 million ($4.14 million) in revenue and income greater than ÷300,000 ($414,000).[56]

According to Italy's solar industry, the result of these and other changes has been a surge in bankruptcies and a massive decrease in solar investment.

EUROPE'S WOOD CONSUMPTION

Besides incentivizing wind and solar generation, EU is also consuming wood to satisfy its renewable mandate of 20 percent of generation from renewable energy by 2020. According to the Economist, wood, the fuel of preindustrial societies, represents about half of all renewable energy consumed in the European Union in some form or another—sticks, pellets, sawdust.[57] In Poland and Finland, for example, wood supplies more than 80 percent of renewable energy demand. In Germany, despite its push and subsidization of wind and solar power, 38 percent of nonfossil fuel consumption comes from wood.

According to the International Wood Markets Group, Europe consumed 13 million metric tons of wood pellets in 2012 and its demand is expected to increase to 25 to 30 million tons a year by 2020. According to the National Firewood Association, the 2012 European consumption of wood pellets is equivalent to over 4 million cords of wood, which equates to over 4 million ''big'' trees and over 8 million ''average size'' trees.[58]

Because Europe does not produce enough timber to meet this demand, imports of wood pellets are increasing. They increased by 50 percent in 2010. According to the European Pellet Council, global trade in wood pellets is expected to increase five- or six-fold to 60 million metric tons by 2020. Much of that will come from new wood-exporting businesses that are booming in western Canada and the southern United States. According to a report by Wood Resources International, the southern United States surpassed Canada last year as the leading exporter of wood pellets to Europe, exporting in excess of 1.5 million tons. Those exports are expected to reach 5.7 million tons in 2015. During the third quarter of 2012, three companies announced plans for new pellet plants in Georgia and six others were under construction in the south, together adding as much as 4.2 million tons of capacity by 2015.[59]

The increase in wood consumption has caused an escalation in prices. According to data published by Argus Biomass Markets, an index of wood-pellet prices increased by 11 percent, from 116 euros ($152) a metric ton in August 2010 to 129 euros ($169) a metric ton at the end of 2012. Since the end of 2011, prices for hardwood from western Canada increased by about 60 percent.[60]

Wood use in Europe, however, is not carbon neutral. In theory, if the biomass used to power electricity comes from energy crops, the carbon generated from combustion would be offset by the carbon that is captured and stored in the newly planted crops, making the process carbon-neutral. The wood that Europe is using produces carbon through combustion at the power station and in the manufacture of the pellets that includes grinding the wood up, turning it into dough and submitting it under pressure. The process of producing the pellets, combusting them, and transporting them produces carbon—about 200 kilograms of carbon dioxide for each megawatt hour of electricity generated.

A researcher at Princeton University calculated that if whole trees are used to produce energy, they would increase carbon emissions compared with coal by 79 percent over 20 years and 49 percent over 40 years and that there would be no carbon reduction for 100 years until the replacement trees have matured.

EUROPE'S NATURAL GAS SUPPLIES

Europe is worried about continually receiving the 30 percent of its natural gas supplies that it receives from Russia, but instead of embracing hydraulic fracturing and horizontal drilling on domestic soil, it is looking toward the United States to export LNG to them. According to a leaked document, the European Union is making its desire to import more oil and natural gas from the United States very clear in the discussions over the Transatlantic Trade and Investment Partnership (TTIP) trade deal. The EU is pressuring the United States to lift its ban on crude oil exports and make it easier to export natural gas to Europe. The EU emphasizes the TTIP's role in ''reinforcing the security of supply'' of energy for the member countries, pointing to the political situation in the Ukraine as a key reason to relax rules against U.S. exports. ''The current crisis in Ukraine confirms the delicate situation faced by the EU with regard to energy dependence,'' the document states. ''Of course the EU will continue working on its own energy security and broaden its strategy of diversification. But such an effort begins with its closest allies.''[61]

EU could start by developing its shale gas resources throughout its member countries. According to the Energy Information Administration, Europe has an estimated 470 trillion cubic feet of technically recoverable shale gas resources, around 80 percent of the U.S. estimated endowment of 567 trillion cubic feet.[62] As previously mentioned, Germany has proposed a prohibition against hydraulic fracturing through 2021. France, which has the second-largest estimated shale gas resources in Europe, has a hydraulic fracturing ban through at least 2017 and Bulgaria also forbids hydraulic fracturing. Poland, which has Europe's largest technically recoverable shale gas resources at 148 trillion cubic feet, is interested in developing those resources, but has geology problems demonstrated by poor results from exploratory drilling. Several other European countries are now interested in developing their shale gas resources, such as the U.K., the Netherlands, Denmark, and Romania, but none of the European shale-gas exploration efforts are close to being ready for commercial development.[63]

CONCLUSION

As the Washington Post indicated: ''Cap-and-trade regimes have advantages, notably the ability to set a limit on emissions and to integrate with other countries. But they are complex and vulnerable to lobbying and special pleading, and they do not guarantee success.''[64]

The European Union has found this to be the case, for their cap-and-trade program did not achieve the intended targets, but made many companies wealthier which in turn resulted in higher energy prices for consumers. Other ''green'' energy programs have had similar results in producing higher electricity prices and large subsidies for technologies that contribute only small amounts to their countries' electricity needs. Countries that have enacted these programs have found them to be very costly and are now slashing those subsidies because the governments and the consumers cannot afford them.

It is unclear what benefit the EU and Australia's climate and ''green'' energy policies have achieved. Any reduction in carbon dioxide emissions that developed countries make will just be a ''drop in the bucket'' because total global greenhouse gas emissions will increase as China, the world's largest emitter of carbon dioxide emissions, and other developing countries continue to improve their economies by using fossil fuels. These developing countries believe it is their turn to develop their economies and to provide energy to their citizens, many of which do not even have electricity. As a result, they either refuse to participate in global climate change programs or have track records of not enforcing such programs.

The climate policies of both Europe and Australia have not only driven up their energy prices, but have also harmed their economies and reduced their security capabilities. Because Europe is dependent on natural gas from Russia, it has secretly asked the United States to speed up its review of LNG applications. Europe is clearly worried about further Russian aggression and availability of its natural gas supplies.

Australia has learned and repealed its carbon tax with Senate approval on July 17. According to Tony Abbott, Australia's Prime Minister, in releasing the news of the passage of the repeal legislation to Australia's citizens, "We are honoring our commitments to you and building a strong and prosperous economy for a safe and secure Australia."[65]

Europe and the United States need to learn that energy security requires energy diversity. For example, during the cold spell in the U.S. Northeast this past winter, natural gas prices spiked because of lack of infrastructure. Lights were kept on due to the availability of coal and nuclear units. But many of those units are now being shuttered, which means that during next winter, the lights may go out in the Northeast.

End Notes

[1] Energy Information Administration, International Energy Data Base.
[2] Ibid.
[3] The Wall Street Journal, Cap and Trade Doesn't Work, June 25, 2009.
[4] The Wall Street Journal, Cap and Trade Doesn't Work, June 25, 2009.
[5] Interpol, Guide to Carbon Trading Crime, June 2013.
[6] The Wall Street Journal, Cap and Trade Doesn't Work, June 25, 2009.
[7] Interpol, Guide to Carbon Trading Crime, June 2013.
[8] Bloomberg, Deutsche Bank, RWE raided in German probe of CO_2 tax, April 28, 2010.
[9] Reuters, Germany seeks arrest of Briton in carbon trading scam, April 10, 2014.
[10] Bloomberg, Deutsche Bank, RWE raided in German probe of CO_2 tax, April 28, 2010.
[11] European Commission, The EU Emissions Trading System.
[12] Defense News, U.S. Pushes NATO Allies to Boost Defense Spending, May 3, 2014.
[13] Huffington Post, Australia's Carbon Tax Set for Final Showdown, July 14, 2014.
[14] Department of the Environment, Australian Government, Repealing the Carbon Tax.
[15] ABC, Senate Passes Legislation to Repeal Carbon Tax, July 17, 2014.
[16] Wall Street Journal, Australia Becomes First Developed Nation to Repeal Carbon Tax, July 17, 2014.
[17] Australia's Carbon Tax: An Economic Evaluation, September 2013.
[18] Institute for Building Efficiency, Feed-In Tariffs: A Brief History.
[19] Financial Post, Governments Rip Up Renewable Contracts, March 19, 2014.
[20] Bloomberg, Spain's Power Deficit Widens by 46 Percent as Steps to Close Gap Founder, April 25, 2014.
[21] Institute for Energy Research, August 6, 2009.
[22] Study of the effects on employment of public aid to renewable energy sources, Universidad Rey Juan Carlos, March 2009.
[23] Eagle Tribune, Cap-and-trade bill is an economy-killer, June 28, 2009.
[24] The Failure of Global Carbon Policies, June 11, 2014.
[25] Spain Youth Unemployment Rises to Record 57.7 Percent, Surpasses Greece, January 8, 2014.
[26] Financial Post, Governments Rip Up Renewable Contracts, March 19, 2014.
[27] Wall Street Journal, "Darker Times for Solar-Power Industry," May 11, 2009.
[28] Heinrich Böll Foundation, Energy Transition: The German Energiewende.
[29] Institute for Building Efficiency, Feed-In Tariffs: A Brief History, Aug. 2010.
[30] German Federal Ministry of Economics and Technology and Ministry for the Environment, Nature Conservation and Nuclear Safety.
[31] Forbes, "Germany's Energy Goes Kaput, Threatening Economic Stability," December 30, 2013.
[32] BP Statistical Review of World Energy 2014.
[33] Wall Street Journal, Germany's fracking follies, July 7, 2014.
[34] Energy Information Administration, Technically Recoverable Shale Oil and Shale Gas Resources: An Assessment of 137 Shale Formations in 41 Countries Outside the United States, June 2013.
[35] Europe's Energy Portal Germany Energy Prices Report.
[36] U.S. Energy Information Administration, Monthly Energy Review.
[37] Tree Hugger, German Electricity Tax Rises 50 Percent to Support Renewable Energy, October 17, 2012.
[38] Reuters, Five million German families faced with higher power bills, February 24, 2014.
[39] Frontier Economics, German renewable energy levy will rise in 2014.
[40] The Australian, Europe Pulls the Plug on its Green Energy Future, August 10, 2013.
[41] New York Times, Germany's Effort at Clean Energy Proves Complex, September 18, 2013.
[42] Renewables International, First municipal offshore wind farm awaits grid connection, June 25, 2014.
[43] Bloomberg, Germany moots levy on renewable power use, February 4, 2014.
[44] Wall Street Journal, Germany's Upper House Passes Renewable Energy Law, July 11, 2014.
[45] Institute for Building Efficiency, Feed-In Tariffs: A Brief History, Aug. 2010.
[46] International Energy Agency, Global Renewable Energy, National Renewable Energy Action Plan.
[47] Bloomberg, Green Rules Shuttering Power Plants Threaten UK Shortage, March 19, 2014.
[48] Bloomberg, Green Rules Shuttering Power Plants Threaten UK Shortage, March 19, 2014.
[49] The Telegraph, Wind farms subsidies cut by 25 percent, July 14, 2013.
[50] The Telegraph, Wind farm plans in tatters after subsidy rethink, March 2, 2014.

61

[51] Mail Online, Solar panel payments are about to fall again but the cost of buying them is falling too—so is it still worth investing?, June 14, 2013.
[52] The Telegraph, Wind farms subsidies cut by 25 percent, July 14, 2013.
[53] The Global Warming Policy Foundation, Proposals to Step up Unilateral Climate Policy Will Trigger ''Astronomical Costs,'' Peiser Warns, July 15, 2014.
[54] International Energy Agency, Global Renewable Energy, ''Old'' Feed In Premium for Photovoltaic Systems.
[55] Bloomberg, Italy Set to Cease Granting Tariffs for New Solar Projects, June 11, 2013.
[56] Financial Post, Governments Rip Up Renewable Contracts, March 18, 2014.
[57] Economist, Wood The Fuel of the Future, April 6, 2013.
[58] National Firewood Association, Biomass Called Environmental Lunacy, April 10, 2013.
[59] Dogwood Alliance, The Use of Whole Trees in Wood Pellet Manufacturing, November 13, 2012.
[60] Argus Biomass Markets.
[61] Huffington Post, Secret Trade Doc Calls for More Oil and Gas Exports to Europe, July 8, 2014.
[62] Energy Information Administration, Technically Recoverable Shale Oil and Shale Gas Resources: An Assessment of 137 Shale Formations in 41 Countries Outside the United States, June 2013.
[63] Europe wants the energy, but not the fracking, July 15, 2014.
[64] The Washington Post, Climate Change Solutions, February 16, 2009.
[65] Australia's carbon tax has been axed as repeal bills clear the Senate, July 17, 2014.

Senator MARKEY. Thank you, Ms. Hutzler. Good to see you again.

She did not say that she agreed with me on everything, but we are old pals from these debates in the past.

Let me just begin by saying I think Senator Murphy and I agree that if there is any crook in any part of the energy sector anywhere in the world, that they should be cuffed, tried, and jailed. So we can agree with that, and it does not make any difference if we are talking about Gazprom or we are talking about Enron or we are talking about anything else that has fraudsters in it. The surest and certain way of policing that is to just make sure that the cops come in and arrest them in front of everybody else, and then the mothers of everyone else are just so ashamed they call their son or daughter and just say: I hope you are not doing the same thing in the energy market. So let us just hope we have cops on the beat.

In addition, I think what I would just like to say is we do have a cap-and-trade system in the United States. We call it the Regional Greenhouse Gas Initiative. It is all of New England plus New York and Maryland and Delaware. There has not been any accusations of rampant corruption. Moreover, we have actually seen a 40-percent reduction in greenhouse gases in that sector over the last 8 years. And, very interestingly, electricity prices have gone down over that same period of time. So I would just like to stipulate that.

Let me begin with you, Admiral Titley. Could you talk a little bit about your own views on climate change and its interrelationship with defense policy? What has happened over the years, in your own thinking?

Admiral TITLEY. Thanks very much, Senator, for that question. It is, I think, a matter of public record: it is on a TED Talk and a number of other places, I actually started out as a pretty big skeptic regarding climate change. I was trained as a meteorologist. I sometimes tell people I am a recovering forecaster. And I lived and died by the computer models. Back when I was going to college, they frankly were not much good more than about 2, maybe 3 days out, probably 2 days out.

When you were running naval oceanography, it was really all weather and it was the tactical side of the ocean. So that is pretty much what I did for quite a long time. The climate continued to change and, by the 2000s, as I was becoming a senior officer, you start looking—we call it looking a little bit beyond the horizon—and you start seeing these issues. ADM Gary Roughead, then Chief of Naval Operations, asked me to come up to Washington from my current job and start running a task force on climate change.

The first thing I did is I kind of fell back on my training as a navigator. I probably have to remind half the people in here, there was a time that we did not have Global Positioning Systems, so I actually had to use a sextant, and you had to use all the data. So that is what I did; I wanted to look at all the data, not trusting any one piece of data entirely.

So I looked at how much radiation are we getting from the sun, how much heat and energy are we getting from the sun? What else could be causing this? Scientists sort of wanted to try to disprove the theory. And you would look at these independent lines of evidence, very similar to how you would navigate a ship: air temperatures, sea temperatures, ocean ice melting, land ice melting, ecosystems moving either Pole-ward or north-ward.

All of this came to support what I call cutting edge, 19th century science, a bunch of old dead white guys. Fourier, Tindall, Arnhus basically had kind of figured out the theory back between 1842 and 1895. We are simply refining that, but that is what it is. And I came to my independent conclusion that that is what we are doing.

So I am sort of like the reformed smoker. I am probably the worst type of climate person here because I started out really not seeing that. If somebody else wants to ask, I can tell people why climate models are good for 30 or 50 years or more, but weather models still have trouble after a few days.

Thank you, sir.

Senator MARKEY. But do you have to be a weatherman to predict that the defense of our Nation is going to be affected by the changes in the climate?

Admiral TITLEY. No, sir, and that is the beauty of the Military Advisory Board: it is comprised of 16 admirals and generals, all except for myself and Royal Navy ADM Neil Morisetti are three and four stars, and none of those three and four stars are either weather or oceanography experts. They are war-fighting admirals and generals. So they deal with the specialty branches, be it logistics, intelligence, and so forth every day in their professional lives. They are paid to make assessments.

What they see is a change in our physical battle space. And, just like the Department of Defense looks at, and war-fighting commanders look at, changes in demographics, economics, political environments, we would frankly be negligent if we did not plan for the chance and for the risk of these changes in the climate. Large consequence, not exactly known probability, but we would be negligent if we said, well, it is not going to happen.

Senator MARKEY. Mr. Breen, a lot of people again say that oil and gas are just the same as any other commodity; it is no different from a computer chip or a watch. And I suppose the Swiss Army might go to war over watches, but I am not sure many other countries would. Can you talk a little bit about that and the special role that oil and gas do play and how we should be viewing that from the perspective of the United States?

Mr. BREEN. Sure, Mr. Chairman. Thanks for the question. I think the difference between oil and gas and other commodities is these energy commodities are strategic commodities. They are things that every advanced economy in the world is dependent on in order to function and survive, that every advanced military needs in order to fight.

For example, oil is a great example of this. The U.S. transportation sector, over 93 percent of our transportation sector is dependent on oil to move. This is, as we all know, it is a globally traded, fungible commodity. There is a highly integrated global market for it, which means that events that happen anywhere in the world affect our supply, which affects in turn, because we are not diversified, I would argue, because we are single source dependent on this one commodity, we are stuck. Whatever happens to the price around the world, whatever happens to supply, we need to respond to that.

That is, frankly, the nightmare that Ukraine finds itself in now. They are dependent on a single massive supplier of resources. As the gentleman from the State Department testified earlier, sir, they are asking themselves if they are going to make it through the winter because they are so dependent on a single strategic commodity for the welfare of their people. That is a geopolitical, strategic, and ultimately military problem, not an economic one.

Senator MARKEY. Thank you.

Senator Barrasso.

Senator BARRASSO. Thank you, Mr. Chairman. Mr. Chairman, Senator Inhofe had a statement that he would like to have included in the record and I ask unanimous consent that I could submit that on his behalf.

Senator MARKEY. Without objection.

Senator BARRASSO. Thank you, Mr. Chairman.

Ms. Hutzler, you cited a number of examples of failed climate policies in Europe, including Germany, Spain, the United Kingdom, Italy. Would you like to elaborate further on these examples? Are there other examples not included in your testimony that you could highlight for us?

Ms. HUTZLER. Certainly. As I mentioned, in each of these cases the government enacted green energy laws, and in order to get the mandates that they wanted they had to subsidize these technologies to a great extent. That increased electricity prices, it hurt their economies, and they lost jobs. So they ended up amending or repealing some of these laws.

The specifics of the different policies are different across the countries, but essentially, like Germany had their residential customers pay more for the subsidies than their industrial customers. They were protecting some of them. In Spain, the government actually took up some of the difference in the subsidies because they did not get enough money from the consumers. In fact, since 2000 Spain paid $41 billion more for the power that they received than their consumers actually paid for. So that puts them pretty much into national debt.

But in each of these cases what we see happening is that they are slashing these subsidies. In Germany's case they are trying to spread the subsidies over more of the businesses rather than just the residential customers.

Senator BARRASSO. Can you tell me how successful the Kyoto Protocol was in making countries that signed the treaty more energy independent and secure from countries or foreign entities that did not share their strategic interests?

Ms. HUTZLER. Well, I do not think that they are more energy independent and secure. It is just the opposite. If you take a look at their energy prices, their electricity price, for instance, as I mentioned, it is 37 percent higher than the U.S. price indexed to 2005 levels. So their policies, in fact, have hurt them.

In one case that I mentioned, they are actually spending less on defense now than they did prior to the Kyoto Protocol. They are spending only 1.6 percent of their GDP. NATO guidance says that they should be spending 2 percent. And we are spending as much as 2.5 percent. In fact, Secretary of Defense Hagel has called on the EU to spend more because of the crisis in the Ukraine.

Senator BARRASSO. Well, that is what I heard when I was in Latvia and Lithuania, that the concerns are that they were supposed to get to 2 percent, but they are unable to, and a lot of it has to do with the expenses that you have outlined. You mentioned them specifically in your report when you talk about the impact on the economies, that they are having to not have the available funds to spend on defense, which is putting a specific additional stress on NATO.

If the United States had adopted a cap-and-trade system, do you think it would have helped or hurt our strategic interests?

Ms. HUTZLER. I personally think that it would hurt them because of the same thing that happened in the European Union. In fact, you can take a look at Australia, who just repealed its carbon tax because it was not globally competitive. Electricity prices increased 15 percent, unemployment went down 10 percent, and it just made them not globally competitive, which is an important part of being energy secure.

Senator BARRASSO. I think it was an interesting discussion and then decision in Australia to repeal because of the specific impacts of it on the economy. Anything else that you kind of gained from that Australian decision?

Ms. HUTZLER. I find it very interesting that it was just in place for 2 years and they recognized this. Their citizens were very unhappy about the fact that they could not compete globally.

Senator BARRASSO. Thank you

Mr. Goldwyn, thanks so much for your report on uncertain energy. In your testimony you state that the United States and other stable democratic countries, such as Canada and Australia, are well poised to meet a considerable share of the world's growing oil and gas demand and attain the associated export revenues. From a geopolitical perspective, you say, increased LNG exports from the United States and its allies would shift rents away from traditional autocratic suppliers, including Russia, that have used the proceeds to finance policies at odds with United States national security interests.

You went on to say a clear signal from the United States that LNG exports will be available to European allies for future purchase would put immediate pressure on Russia's market share and export revenues.

Do you believe United States liquified natural gas exports can serve as this important diplomatic tool for the United States to strengthen our national security and to assist the security of our allies and helping to alleviate manipulations and threats from Russia, and could you expand on that a little bit?

Mr. GOLDWYN. Yes, sir, I do. I think that our ability to export LNG is an important foreign policy tool. First, we increase the global supply of LNG. We bring down the price. We make it more accessible. When the price goes down, our competitors will lose revenue, and right now Russia is a major, major exporter of gas. We saw the historical example of this when over the last few years, when the displacement of LNG meant for the U.S. forced Gazprom to renegotiate most of its contracts with Europe and forced them to power prices.

It is also forcing the delinkage between the pricing of gas correlating to the price of oil and having gas correlate to its more natural competitor, which is coal. So I think there is a price benefit and there is also a supply benefit. Both countries in Europe and Asia want secure suppliers. Often they will pay a premium for knowing that they have a secure source of supply. So our willingness to export to them, as seen by the initial contracts even for the projects right now, show that countries in Europe and Asia are interested in that.

Third, to the extent that they buy from us and they do not buy from somebody else, those rents go here, they do not go elsewhere. Numerous studies, the study on net benefits for the Department of Energy, the Brookings study on LNG exports, the DeLoitte study which is cited in I think the testimony I had before the Energy and Natural Resources, show that just the swap on LNG is almost a $4 billion shift away from Russia to European consumers by bringing down those prices.

So there is a lot of benefits, and it is a little bit of practicing what we preach, too. For years we have been building a system based on global trade. We have relied on that to get resources when we need them. It is just a little bit of practice what you preach.

Senator BARRASSO. Thank you.

Thank you very much, Mr. Chairman. My time has expired.

Senator MARKEY. Thank you.

Well, we will go to a second round. We just have an incredible panel here. I think it is important—thank you, Mr. Breen, for raising the question of what happens with oil production in the United States, because even though we still import 30 percent of the oil that we consume in the United States, there are advocates for us to start exporting, even though we still import 30 percent and even though, as you are saying, the Energy Information Agency is saying we are going to plateau relatively soon in terms of our total oil production.

So that goes to a national security issue, too: How wise are we to be exporting our own oil and natural gas when we do not have a surplus today and production is going to slow down and plateau in the relatively near future? Can you talk about that?

Mr. BREEN. Sure, Chairman, and thank you. I think the question really to me is how do you make use of opportunity. If you end up in a situation where you have, as Ms. Hutzler said, an unexpected increase in supply, which is likely to increase in production, which is unlikely to last all that long into the future, how do you make use of that? I would argue that there are a number of things we could do domestically with natural gas supplies that might be extremely beneficial.

For example, transitioning municipal truck fleets, garbage trucks, buses, things like that to natural gas might help alleviate our single-source dependence on oil to fuel our transportation sector, which I would argue is a strategic risk, being so dependent on oil for that purpose.

Senator MARKEY. I think that there is another canard out there that renewable electricity is not working on the planet, whereas the reality is that last year 50 percent—listen to this: 50 percent of all new electrical generating capacity for the world was renewable, 50 percent of all new capacity installed last year. So we can pick out individual places if we want, but that is a pretty big trend across the planet, even in the United States.

We can go back—you can talk about Spain, but let us talk about the United States. When President Bush left office the Dow was at 7,000, unemployment was at 10 percent. Since President Obama's been in office, we have installed 70,000 megawatts of wind and solar in our country and by the end of next year we could be—maybe the end of 2016, we will have 100,000 megawatts of wind and solar in the United States, which is equal to the nuclear power industry after 60 years. And over that same period of time, during the Obama administration, the Dow went from 7,000 to 17,000, the unemployment rate has gone from 10 percent down to 6 percent.

So I do not think we should be looking at Spain. We should be looking at ourselves. The same thing is true with the Regional Greenhouse Gas Initiative, the cap-and-trade system we have for the utility sector across the Northeast. Greenhouse gases went down by 40 percent, electricity rates went down, and we saw a massive installation actually of renewable energy plus conservation, energy efficiency.

So can you talk about that global perspective, Admiral Titley, and how you view this revolution and what we should be doing as a nation to kind of encourage that indigenous installation of renewables, energy efficiency, self-sufficiency in other words, in other countries of the world?

Admiral TITLEY. Thanks, Senator. Really, the way I take a look at this as a risk-based issue, so how do we mitigate the risks of the climate change? We talk in our MAB report about stabilizing the climate. Clearly, one way to help stabilize the climate is to reduce the amount of carbon that you are putting into the air. It is kind of like for 150 years we have just been sort of dumping the trash out in the road and nobody has picked it up, so we do not either stop dumping trash and we do not even put it back in the ground.

So the more we can do on these types of renewables, I think we are in good shape. I am often asked, do I believe in climate change? And I tell people, no, I do not believe in climate change. I am convinced by the evidence that it is happening. What I do believe in is American ingenuity. I think that—and I end just about every talk I give with, actually it is a slide out of the Tom Hanks' Apollo 13 movie, where we get the guys back against all odds—this country, when focused, can do incredible things.

So if we can, through the help of the Congress, Sir, set the right incentives, set the right certainty, the ingenuity in the academic, private, and government sectors will come together and we will fix this problem. We really can fix this problem. The examples you gave, sir, are just the leading edge of how we can do this. We will get there. It is how much pain are we going to suffer.

Ms. HUTZLER. Senator Markey——

Senator MARKEY. Excuse me just a minute. The reality is that Tom Hanks was right in the Apollo movie. Failure is not an option. They had to innovate. They had to be imaginative. They had to figure out a way of improvising in order to get that capsule back to Earth.

The same thing is true for us right now, except it is the entire planet, and failure is not an option because we know that the worst, most catastrophic impacts are coming and it is going to have a devastating impact upon our national security and the globe's.

I do believe they are weapons of mass destruction, these storms. I mean, when the U.S. Congress is talking about appropriately $60 billion in the aftermath of Hurricane Sandy. That is quite a catastrophe that we had to appropriate money in order to deal with. It would have been in a lot of ways smarter to spend the money up front in avoiding the worst consequences, because we would have jobs, we would have industries, and we would have things that we could export around the world as well.

So from my perspective—and I will just give you one final shot at this, Admiral. Can you just talk a little bit about how concerned should the Nation be about this issue? Can you just go to that? How do these 16 admirals and generals that you represent here today view this as a threat to us?

Admiral TITLEY. Yes, Sir, thank you. We see this, frankly, as an accelerating risk for national security. It is like, well, what does that mean? Really, what we see is this change on which we have literally built human civilization. If you take a look at how the climate has varied, and it varies a tremendous amount—people say, well, it changed before, it will change again. Absolutely. But about 8 to 10,000 years ago, after we came out of the Ice Age, it stabilized. When did we get agriculture? When did we literally get the first civilization? And the next thing you know we are all carrying around iPhones and looking at them. That all happened on the basis of our not having had to spend effort to move about.

That is, we have done tremendous things with fossil fuels. Look at the kind of life these have given us. The unintended byproduct, though, is that those have, in fact, jeopardized that very foundational basis on which we have built our civilization. So we have got to figure out how to at least keep or improve our life. And we can do that. We can have a better life even than what we have right now, but at the same time stop this harmful effect.

And if we do not do that, that is where we see these risks. Some people talk about humanitarian assistance, disaster relief, and that is all well and good. I am more concerned about these varsity-level impacts, what we are starting to see now in North Africa, ISIS—we have already talked about this. These really unintended scary consequences come out that can be traced back to a thread, not the cause but a thread, going back to climate, Sir.

Senator MARKEY. Thank you very much.

Senator Barrasso.

Senator BARRASSO. Ms. Hutzler, I think there were some things you might have wanted to add in on that?

Ms. HUTZLER. Yes. I wanted to address some of the remarks that Senator Markey made. He talked about a certain measure in electricity generation and that is capacity. He did not talk about generation. And he compared 100 gigawatts of renewables to 100 gigawatts of nuclear. Well, if you take nuclear, it has a capacity factor of 90 percent. Renewables have a capacity factor, such as wind, around 30 percent.

So in that 100 gigawatts capacity, you are going to be generating three times as much more electricity from nuclear than you are from renewables. They are just not comparable.

I also wanted to address his comments regarding the Regional Greenhouse Gas Initiative, lowering greenhouse gas emissions and lowering electricity prices. Well, first of all, greenhouse gas emissions were lowered after 2008 because of the global recession. That was one of the biggest impacts of lowering carbon dioxide emissions.

Another is the whole shale revolution, where we used hydraulic fracturing and horizontal drilling to get natural gas. That dropped natural gas prices down to about a fourth and that really reduced the cost of generating electricity. So actually natural gas combined cycle units are the cheapest form of technology that you can use to generate electricity and actually get electricity from it.

But I also wanted to mention the issue in Senator Markey's home State of Cape Wind, offshore wind. Cape Wind has been trying to get both the financing and the customers to build the wind farm offshore for now over a decade. They think they finally have it together. But that wind is going to cost the people in Massachusetts 18 cents per kilowatt hour just to start. Then under the 15-year contract it goes up by 3.5 percent a year, so it is going to end up 25 cents a kilowatt hour. That is two and a half times what we pay for the average cost of electricity in this country.

So you have to be very cautious about which renewable technologies you pick, both in terms of the amount of generation you can get from them and from their cost.

Senator BARRASSO. I wanted to ask one other thing. You heard my questioning of the first panel about this increasing manipulation of the European carbon reduction policies and the funding of international crime groups. Do you view this as a serious flaw in carbon trading schemes and other climate-inspired policies, and do you see some serious unintended consequences to our own national security if the United States adopts such policies as those that were taken in Europe?

Ms. HUTZLER. Well, carbon trading policies are very complex. They are complex because of the number of participants and they are complex because they have components that are very difficult to implement right. As a result, you can get a lot of unintended consequences, as I mentioned in my testimony. Certainly one of the criminal activities—and yes, there are criminal activities everywhere, but I think you see a lot more in a carbon trading scheme than you do in a carbon tax, as in Australia's situation. The complexity is very different.

Another place where we have seen abuse in the United States is with renewable identification numbers. Refiners have to use so much biofuels when they produce gasoline, and so on and so forth, their products, and there has been abuse there where there have been fake RIN's that these people have purchased and we have actually gotten these people—we have found most of this fraud. So it is happening in this country, too, when you have a policy like that.

Senator BARRASSO. Thank you.

Mr. Goldwyn, if I could just get back to our Latin American energy needs. In your report, Latin America and the Caribbean region have incredibly high energy costs and insufficient rates of investment. Many of the countries rely upon energy sources such as Venezuela oil which may not be sustainable in the long run. So we see greater energy diversification for these countries as something that would be important for them.

U.S. natural gas exports as part of that broader energy strategy I believe can help nations in the Western Hemisphere as well, to help them lower energy costs to consumers, to businesses, to enhance competitiveness, promote economic growth, provide jobs here at home as well. In your testimony you noted that, ''Promoting the adoption of gas in the Caribbean and Central American energy mix would bring about several benefits for U.S. interests.'' Could you just expand a little bit about what are the benefits to the United States and what impacts U.S. exports of liquified natural gas would have on the region and its energy needs?

Mr. GOLDWYN. Sure. Thank you, Senator, and I want to give credit to the Inter-American Development Bank. They actually did a prefeasibility study on the availability of gas for the region and they are the ones that came up with these calculations that the average price of electricity in the top 12 economies is over 30 cents per kilowatt, the average in the United States is about a dime, and seeing the climate and economic benefits of substituting gas for fuel oil and diesel.

So the benefits are several. The region is important to us. Economically, it is closely tied to South Florida's tourism industry. For migration purposes, stable populations are important. Certainly if there was instability in that region, Jamaica, Dominican Republic, they would be much more vulnerable to transnational crime. And for moral reasons, these are our neighbors.

So for them to have competitive economies they have to have affordable electricity. For them to deal with climate change, they need to have a smaller carbon footprint than they have right now. And for them to have political autonomy, they need to have liberation from dependence on Venezuela for the credit with which they buy all of their oil and their product. So all of those are tremendous benefits to the United States if we are able to help them and we can do it at a relatively low cost.

The long-term solution for these countries—and they have great potential for renewable energy, some geothermal, some wind, some solar. But the intermittency problem is significant for them. They have to have baseload electricity. This is the problem worldwide, is where do you get baseload electricity? You have got coal, oil, nuclear, and gas. And for significant near-term greenhouse gas reduction, gas is actually the most cost-effective scaleable alternative.

If I could, Senator, there has been a lot of talk about whether oil is a strategic commodity and what we should do about it. I would just like to address that. There is no question that oil and good are both strategic commodities. We would never think of banning the export of food, particularly to other countries, because we needed to, it was a strategic commodity and we needed to keep it at home. I think the same is true of oil and of gas. If we—the fact that we import some and we do not—and we import basically heavy oil, which matches our refineries, but we no longer import light oil because we produce so much we have it in surplus, does not mean that we should not export it.

It is the basic principle of comparative advantage. If we can sell something and make more money and put that into the economy, then why not? And if the day comes, frankly, when we do not have it in surplus, the economics will not justify exporting it and we will go back to doing what we have done for decades, which is asking other countries to produce as much as they can and not to restrict the export, to allow the global market to move it to its most efficient source.

So we will need that insurance. The question is now, today, when we have a surplus, why should we not do what we have asked every other country in the world to do and when we can do it in an efficient way and benefit ourselves? I think that is an element of contradiction, is a nice word. But we are in the middle of negotiating two major trade agreements. I think it is really important that we practice what we preach.

Senator BARRASSO. Thank you.

Thank you, Mr. Chairman.

Senator MARKEY. The chair would recognize himself again, just to say this: that if we had a 30-percent shortage of wheat in the United States, and people said, well, we should export part of that 70 percent that we still have, I do not think America would be happy with that. I do not think they would say, let us export wheat even though we are importing 30 percent of the wheat that we use in our country right now, and there might be a little part of the country that has a little surplus, let us send it out of the country. I think that we would not export it, Mr. Goldwyn. That is what I think.

I agree with you that food and oil are in the same category, but the fact that we have a surplus of food puts us in a different category than we have with our energy resources, where we do not have a surplus. We are still importing. So it is just a different situation.

If you remember, Russia stopped exporting wheat when they had a problem, when they had a drought. They just stopped exporting it, because wheat is like oil. They are not sending their extra wheat into the Ukraine. They are sending extra wheat into the Ukraine when they had a shortage.

So from my perspective, I put those two in the same category. And I think it is a good analogy, food and oil and natural gas. In each instance, when we do not have a surplus and when it is a big deficit, which it is with oil, then I do not think that we should be exporting it.

So here is what I think we should do, give each of you 1 minute to summarize what it is that you want the committee to know. We will go in reverse order from the opening statements. So we will begin with you, Ms. Hutzler. Give us your 1-minute summary that you would like the committee to remember.

Ms. HUTZLER. I want the committee to remember that Europe's policies in these areas have failed, that they have enacted green energy laws that needed huge subsidies and that their electricity prices increased, that they have lost jobs, and that they have had to amend these laws, and that it has cost them national debt, it has caused corruption and fraud to occur; and that Australia, too, had a carbon tax that they have repealed because of not being competitive in the global marketplace.

Senator MARKEY. Thank you, Ms. Hutzler.

Mr. Breen, you have 1 minute.

Mr. BREEN. Thank you, Mr. Chairman. If I were to summarize, I would say simply that the subject of this hearing and the timing of it are quite appropriate. Energy and security are inextricably intertwined, and the lack of diversification of U.S. supplies and global supplies and sources continues to create opportunities for rivals and adversaries and vulnerabilities for ourselves; that in the face of that and in the face of the reality that in the long term almost all projections that I am aware of do not see increasing U.S. production keeping up with global demand to the extent that it changes the geopolitical calculus for the United States, that in that world the soundest investments are investments in efficiency and investments in more diversified sources of energy, both for ourselves and as a tool of foreign policy for our allies.

I think it is all well and good to export, if you happen to have it, an excess of natural resources. But America's truest contribution to the world, to our allies, and our best export is technical knowledge and innovation.

Senator MARKEY. Thank you, Mr. Breen.

Mr. Goldwyn.

Mr. GOLDWYN. Thank you, Mr. Chairman. Four points. First, we have lots of tools at our disposal to address these energy and climate issues: diplomacy, technical assistance, and open trade. We are going to need to use all of them to address the security challenges we face overseas.

Third, I would say that many of the challenges that we face can be addressed in ways that will both reduce greenhouse gas emissions and increase our security.

But fourth, we need to consider open trade as part of that. Not all is the same and not all—so there are elements that we do not need, which we can export and share with others. The question is when we have something in surplus will we share it with our friends and allies. No country has ever grown its supply of anything by restricting its export. So I think it is something that requires some study, but I urge you to consider.

Senator MARKEY. Thank you, Mr. Goldwyn.

Admiral Titley.

Admiral TITLEY. Thank you, Senator. I would say, as far as the science of climate goes, we do not know everything, but we know an awful lot. If the intelligence community could tell us as much as the climate community can about the next 30 to 50 years, we would find General Clapper and his Agency heads and we would give them all Medals of Freedom today. That is how much we know about climate.

In the military, as General Sullivan famously says, we do not wait for 100 percent certainty to tackle any issue. If you wait for that on the battlefield, you will probably be dead.

With respect to climate, this is really about the food, energy, water, and the nexus of the three very, very critical issues. If they are mishandled in other countries and other regions, that produces stress and that almost always ends up in a poor security situation that the United States usually gets to deal with in some way, shape, or form. We can deal with this in risk management and ulti-mately, sir, America can lead the way. We can fix this.

Thank you.

Senator MARKEY. Thank you, Admiral.

Thank you each for your service here in the Congress. We very much appreciate your testimony here today.

I ask unanimous consent that the record remain open for written questions from committee members to our witnesses until Friday at noon. Without objection, that will be put in the record and any of the answers which you give us in writing to those questions will be seen in the record.

We thank each of you for your testimony today, and we thank everybody else for participating. This hearing is adjourned.

[Whereupon, at 5:05 p.m., the hearing was adjourned.]

ADDITIONAL MATERIAL SUBMITTED FOR THE RECORD

PREPARED STATEMENT OF HON. JAMES M. INHOFE, U.S. SENATOR FROM OKLAHOMA

President Obama and his administration have been aggressively pursuing regula-tions that are damaging to our economy and put future job opportunities at risk for all Americans. The President has also been encouraging the international adoption of these same regulations, particularly as they relate to reducing emissions of green-house gases.

Of all the regulations being pursued by the President, these are the most expen-sive and damaging to economic growth. Study after study has shown that wide-spread regulation of greenhouse gases in the United States would cost the economy anywhere from $300 billion to $400 billion per year. The administration's recently proposed greenhouse gas regulations for power plants are estimated to cost tens of billions of dollars per year, but because these represent only the beginning of the President's regulatory plans, their cost represents only the tip of the iceberg.

Regulations by the Environmental Protection Agency threaten the reality and affordability of our electricity grid, will weaken our economy, and drive more people into the unemployment lines. In a Senate Environment and Public Works Com-mittee hearing on May 14, 2014, committee witness, Marvin Fertel, president and chief executive officer of the Nuclear Energy Institute, testified that government regulations are ''shutting down the backbone of our electricity system.'' With these facts in mind, it is no surprise that recent polls, such as those by Gallup and Pew showing that Americans are uninterested in climate change policy issues.

The U.S. economy is already well developed, and we know how badly these policies will hurt us. If we force the same regulations on underdeveloped nations, like those in Africa, the impact will be devastating. They will not be able to grow their way out of poverty, as many are doing today with access to inexpensive, reliable electricity.

Giving developing countries greater access to inexpensive power was the driving force behind bills in Congress that reformed our international assistance programs. These impoverished countries want to build power plants, but right now that has been made more difficult by existing policies at the Export-Import Bank and the Overseas Private Investment Corporation, which limit their ability to support projects that may increase greenhouse gas emissions. Few developing countries have the technology and money needed to support a growing economy, thirsty for power, while abiding by these regulations and competing in the global marketplace. It should be our policy to help these nations develop—we should not shackle them with environmental regulations the developed world is not itself willing to follow.

Earlier this year the Obama administration submitted its liberal agenda for the United Nations Climate Change Conference in Paris in 2015, which would require all governments to set new targets to drive down greenhouse gas emissions after 2020. This treaty, however, would rely on countries' domestic authorities to enforce their contributions, and we know that countries such as China, Russia, and India will not do anything about it. They are understandably unwilling to sacrifice their economies for the sake of global warming. This unwillingness to implement economically damaging policies is also extending to the developed world. Just last week Australia repealed its much-hated carbon tax, and because of the Australian Prime Minister's leadership to help the poor and those on fixed incomes (who suffer when energy prices needlessly rise), the Australian economy will now save $9 billion AUD per year. This will help spur economic growth there, create jobs and improve the lives of everyone.

We are seeing that there is no real political will—here or abroad—to implement global warming policies. Rather than pushing these unappealing policies on our friends across the globe, when thinking about international energy policy, the President and his administration should be looking to solve real problems by expanding Liquefied Natural Gas (LNG) exports and ramping up energy development at home to bolster the supplies of our allies abroad. These are the things that need to be done in the midst of an increasingly aggressive world. For example, the European Union's ability to apply strong sanctions against the oil and gas industry in Russia, in response to its aggressive actions in Ukraine and Eastern Europe, is restrained by their dependence on the Russian oil and gas industry to supply their energy needs. The United States is the largest natural gas producer in the world; LNG exports from the United States to the European Union could free the European Union of these chains, allowing them to place real economic pressure on Russia to discourage their continued aggression in the region.

The President's willingness to follow through on climate change policies, despite the widespread unpopularity across the globe, underscore the real motivation behind his actions: pleasing his donor base. The Obama administration's agenda must be seen for what it is: a scheme motivated solely by politics with little regard for the American or global consumers. The United States has long been a nation of abundant domestic energy in all its forms, and because of that we have held tremendous advantages over the rest of the world. Instead of regulating and placing impossible restrictions on the undeveloped energy sectors of the developing nations, we should be encouraging growth so that they may compete in the international marketplace, create jobs, and emerge out of poverty.

––––––––

RESPONSES OF AMOS HOCHSTEIN TO QUESTIONS
SUBMITTED BY SENATOR EDWARD J. MARKEY

Question. Does your agency have the information and resources needed to understand and integrate the impacts of climate change on its mission? If not, what is needed?

Answer. The mission of the Bureau of Energy Resources crosses multiple timeframes, from the short-term imperatives of today's geopolitics and ensuring global energy markets are well supplied, to the long-term issues surrounding energy transformation. To the extent that each of these issues is impacted by climate change, our informational limits are analogous to those of the broader scientific community as it continually strives to improve knowledge of discrete climate impacts.

Question. How does the Bureau of Energy Resources incorporate the carbon pollution profile of energy sources into its energy diplomacy work?

Answer. The Bureau of Energy Resources' (ENR) diplomacy focuses on issues that facilitate deployment of low carbon and renewable energy production worldwide in several distinct ways:

(1) ENR supports governments that wish to improve their energy security through energy policy dialogues and technical assistance. Both are aimed at diversifying fuel mix, and encouraging incorporation of low carbon fuels, renewable energy and energy efficiency measures;

(2) ENR supports sharing U.S. experiences and best practices with emerging hydrocarbon producers to develop economically sustainable natural gas resources;

(3) ENR addresses policy and regulatory barriers that inhibit investment in clean energy, while working with development and commercial banks to mobilize finance in the clean energy sector and assist U.S. clean energy companies and equipment suppliers better compete in emerging markets.

Question. How does the Bureau of Energy Resources incorporate the water use profile of energy sources and climate change impacts on water sources into its energy diplomacy work?

Answer. The Bureau of Energy Resources (ENR) works closely with the Bureau of Oceans and International Environmental and Scientific Affairs (OES) Office of Conservation and Water (ECW) to incorporate resource and environmental considerations into our diplomatic engagement. Water availability and management is critical to the function and economic viability of many energy projects, and we address those issues on a case-by-case basis.

When water availability and management is identified as an important issue affecting project or regional success, ENR works with ECW to recommend actions aligned with international best practices. To date, this guidance has ranged from encouraging reinjection of condensed steam at geothermal sites to ensure long-term stability of the thermal reservoir while mitigating the impact of energy development on local surface-water supplies, to advocating for dry-cooling of large thermal cycles.

Question. Your testimony noted that new non-OPEC oil producers are becoming major energy suppliers. But does not OPEC still control most or all spare oil production capacity in the world? What does that mean in terms of OPEC's ability to continue to influence supply and global oil prices?

Answer. It is true that the Organization of Petroleum Exporting Countries (OPEC) still controls about 2 million barrels per day of spare production capacity, according to U.S. Energy Information Administration estimates. Almost all of this capacity is in Saudi Arabia. However, burgeoning non-OPEC supply tests OPEC's ability to work in concert to decrease rather than increase production. OPEC's unity has recently been shaken as major producers have proven unwilling to unilaterally decrease output and lose market share. This has caused prices to be determined more by market forces rather than OPEC decisions on quotas.

Question. Does the State Department look at the overlap of climate vulnerability/impact and political stability? For example, does the agency look at scenarios like the 2011 wheat crop failures and consider the ramifications in terms of the unrest it could generate in wheat importing nations? Is this the change of regional bureaus or who is responsible for considering these types of issues?

Answer. There are multiple bureaus with the Department of State that examine the relationship between climate vulnerability/impact and political stability. The Department's Office of the Special Envoy for Climate Change (S/SECC) and Bureau of Oceans and International Environmental and Scientific Affairs (OES) look at the overlap between climate change vulnerability and political stability, keeping up to date on emerging scientific issues, and considering these when designing programs and working with partners. The Office of the Chief Economist works closely with the Under Secretary for Economic Growth, Energy and the Environment to examine economic policies that reduce climate vulnerability. The Bureau of Intelligence and Research (INR) also looks at the overlap between climate and political stability, in the context of a range of factors, as part of its engagement with the broader intelligence community.

S/SECC, OES, the Office of the Chief Economist and INR also draw on expertise outside the State Department. Through the new QDDR, and in response to the President's Executive order issued in September 2014 to mainstream climate resilience into agency planning, programs and strategies, the Department has an opportunity to further improve its capacity to consider climate change impacts on security and stability.

Question. Ukraine's reliance on Russian natural gas to meet half of its domestic needs has left it vulnerable to predatory Russian practices in terms of energy supply manipulation. Yet Ukraine has vast untapped domestic natural gas supplies and it is also the second least energy efficient country in the world. I have introduced legislation—S. 2433—that aims to double U.S. governmentwide energy assistance to Ukraine to help them increase efficiency, develop their own resources, and get off Russian gas.

◆   Do you support this legislation? Please provide any thoughts or technical feed- back about this legislation.

Answer. The State Department agrees that Ukraine's reliance on Russian natural gas has left it vulnerable; Ukraine has significant untapped natural gas resources and is woefully energy inefficient. In response to the crisis stemming from Russian aggression in eastern Ukraine, the United States Government has nearly tripled our energy assistance to Ukraine over the past year. This assistance is focused on promoting energy security through support for energy efficiency and diversification of energy sources, as well as improving transparency in the energy sector, which will be crucial to Ukraine establishing a modern, productive energy sector.

The Bureau of Energy Resources' assistance programs are helping Ukraine to sustainably develop its conventional and unconventional gas resources. Specific current engagement includes providing an engineering assessment of gas field surface facilities to eliminate bottlenecks and improve efficiency in existing gas production and instilling best practices in legal, regulatory, environmental, permitting and sustainable development of unconventional gas resources. Planned future engagement includes supporting a competitive international tender for rehabilitation of existing gas fields and advising on a seismic survey in western Ukraine and a subsequent tender for the new oil and gas fields identified Not only will this assistance potentially increase production and reduce dependence on Russian resources, but it will also reduce the gas import bill and the costs of gas production inefficieny, while boosting domestic economic growth and incentivizing foreign direct investment. In parallel the Bureau is currently assisting in the reform of Ukraine's national oil and gas company, Naftogaz, to improve corporate governance and transparency, including at Naftogaz's upstream gas subsidiary, Ukrgasvydobuvannya. It is hoped that this assistance and the reforms and energy efficiency they support will strengthen Ukrainian energy security in the near term and long term. We support efforts to provide additional U.S. foreign assistance to improve energy security in Ukraine.

————

RESPONSES OF DR. DANIEL Y. CHIU TO QUESTIONS
SUBMITTED BY SENATOR EDWARD J. MARKEY

ACCESS TO NECESSARY INFORMATION AND RESOURCES

Question. Does your agency have the information and resources needed to understand and integrate the impacts of climate change on its mission? If not, what is needed?

Answer. The Department bases our response to the effects of climate change on the best data available; as the scientific community's understanding of climate trends develops, we will continue to monitor these changes. The Department has the resources that we need at present. To be best prepared, we are conducting a baseline survey of all DOD sites to identify areas that are mostly likely to be affected by climate change. This survey will enable the Military Departments and defense agencies to identify sites that require additional assessment. As we build on our understanding and identify solutions, we look forward to working with Congress to address any gaps that emerge.

INTEGRATING CLIMATE CHANGE IMPACTS INTO ALLIED MILITARY PLANNING

Question. To what extent are the impacts of climate change being incorporated into the military planning of our allies and military cooperation organizations like NATO?

Answer. Many U.S. allies and partners have identified climate change as a security threat and are conducting a range of planning and resilience activities to address it. The form these preparations take varies by country, given the different effect climate change has in different parts of the world. Some allies and partners have integrated climate change into their national planning documents, some have established dedicated climate change offices, and others address climate change as one key issue among many. Dialogue with our allies and partners has revealed that many view climate change as an emerging and significant challenge, and the Department is committed to further international cooperation on adaptation and planning to meet that challenge.

TRAINING FOR ENVIRONMENTAL SECURITY AND DISASTER PREPAREDNESS COOPERATION

Question. Does DOD incorporate environmental security and disaster preparedness into their training cooperation efforts with other countries' militaries?

Answer. Yes. The Department has long engaged with foreign militaries to enhance resilience and improve our collective readiness for disasters. These efforts include DOD meetings with military planners from Australia, Canada, Korea, Thailand, the Philippines, as well as with military planners from South and Central America. For some countries, planning for natural disasters is an existential issue, while for others it is a form of due diligence. We will continue this cooperation and share best practices to enhance environmental security and plan for disasters.

UKRAINIAN RELIANCE ON RUSSIAN NATURAL GAS

Question. Ukraine's reliance on Russian natural gas to meet half of its domestic needs has left it vulnerable to predatory Russian practices in terms of energy supply manipulation. Yet Ukraine has vast untapped domestic natural gas supplies and it is also the second least energy efficient country in the world. I have introduced legislation—S. 2433—that aims to double U.S. Government-wide energy assistance to Ukraine to help them increase efficiency, develop their own resources, and get off Russian gas.

◆ Do you support this legislation? Please provide any thoughts or technical feed- back about this legislation.

Answer. As the provisions of your bill are beyond the purview of the Defense Department, I defer to other U.S. departments and agencies to assess the bill's technical aspects. In terms of security, Russia has acted in disruptive and irresponsible ways, and the Department broadly supports efforts—including changes in the supply and use of energy—to mitigate the harmful effects of Russia's actions and to enhance Ukraine's energy security.

————

RESPONSES OF RAD DAVID TITLEY TO QUESTIONS
SUBMITTED BY SENATOR EDWARD J. MARKEY

Question. In your testimony you noted that the U.S. needs to prepare for the rapid changes happening in the Arctic. What capabilities and capacities should the United States be prioritizing to be ready for the ongoing changes in the Arctic?

Answer. First and foremost, CNA's Military Advisory Board (MAB) recommends that, in order to expedite crisis response and requirements generation, the Arctic region should be assigned to one Combatant Commander. Second, to provide the United States with better standing to resolve future disputes in the Arctic, the U.S. should become a signatory to the U.N. Convention on the Law of the Sea (UNCLOS).

Although the MAB did not take a position or prioritize specific capabilities, it is "particularly concerned that increased capability is required today to communicate reliably and to conduct search and rescue. We need better charts and aids for navigation, communications capability, enhanced disaster response capabilities, and the ability to exercise freedom of navigation," (i.e., hardened combatants and ice breakers), as noted in its most recent report.

Question. During the hearing, you briefly mentioned that you have more confidence in long-term climate models than in weather forecasts that go beyond 10 days or so. Can you explain why that is?

Answer. Weather forecasts and weather forecasting models are generated with the goal of predicting the exact temperatures, precipitation type and amount, and other weather at a precise point and time. When we assess these forecasts, we compare these predictions to the average weather (climatology) to determine which came closer for that location and time. In general, in the short term, weather forecasts outperform climatology. However, beyond roughly 10 days, these forecasts and forecast models become less accurate than climatology.

Weather forecasts are critically dependent on exact "starting" (or initial) conditions of the atmosphere. For example, to predict the temperature or rainfall in Washington, DC, 1 or 2 days in advance, it is extremely important to know today's weather conditions in the Midwest and southern U.S.

Climate forecasts, by contrast, have virtually no dependence on the exact weather conditions of any given location or day. It would be possible to start a climate model with today's temperatures in Washington, DC, whether 50 degrees or 90 degrees, and still get the correct answer for average summer temperatures—years and decades hence, providing the model correctly represents the amount of heat (or boundary conditions) received by the sun, and how that heat is then distributed and redistributed between the ocean, atmosphere, land, and ice.

Climate models and forecasts are generated with the goal of accurately representing the statistics of the weather (climate) over a broad region. When we assess these models, we are determining if the models can reproduce the average weather as well as the frequency of rare or extreme weather events. In essence, we are not looking to see whether the models can reproduce the precise temperatures at one location on August 5, but whether the models can reproduce the average August temperatures over the last 150 years, as well as the change in average August temperatures over the last 150 years over a large region. In general, the climate models do an accurate job of representing the mean, trends, and other statistics over the past 150 years, so we have confidence that the future model predictions are accurate.

References

AMS Policy Statement on Weather Analysis and Forecasting. Bull. Amer. Met. Soc., 79, 2161–2163 (https://www.ametsoc.org/policy/statewaf.html).

Flato, G., J. Marotzke, B. Abiodun, P. Braconnot, S.C. Chou, W. Collins, P. Cox, F. Driouech, S. Emori, V. Eyring, C. Forest, P. Gleckler, E. Guilyardi, C. Jakob, V. Kattsov, C. Reason and M. Rummukainen, 2013: Evaluation of Climate Models. In: Climate Change 2013: The Physical Science Basis. Contribution of Working Group I to the Fifth Assessment Report of the Intergovernmental Panel on Climate Change [Stocker, T.F., D. Qin, G.-K. Plattner, M. Tignor, S.K. Allen, J. Boschung, A. Nauels, Y. Xia, V. Bex and P.M. Midgley (eds.)]. Cambridge University Press, Cambridge, United Kingdom and New York, NY, USA.

Question. Ukraine's reliance on Russian natural gas to meet half of its domestic needs has left it vulnerable to predatory Russian practices in terms of energy supply manipulation. Yet Ukraine has vast untapped domestic natural gas supplies and it is also the second-least energy efficient country in the world. I have introduced legislation—S. 2433—that aims to double U.S. Government-wide energy assistance to Ukraine to help them increase efficiency, develop their own resources, and get off Russian gas. Do you support this legislation? Please provide any thoughts or technical feedback about this legislation.

Answer. This question is beyond the scope of the work conducted by CNA's Military Advisory Board.

————

RESPONSES OF MARY J. HUTZLER TO QUESTIONS
SUBMITTED BY SENATOR EDWARD J. MARKEY

I have responded to each of the questions from Senator Markey below. I would like to make it clear at the outset that I am in favor of all energy technologies. However, I believe that the energy marketplace should determine the market penetration of each technology, not government policies that distort the economics of the technologies and end up costing the American public more than necessary to pay for the power that they need.

Further, I would note that some of the policies that Senator Markey seems to advocate in his questions below would reduce U.S. energy production, increase oil imports and our trade deficit, and have the effect of reducing U.S. energy security. Senator Markey should understand the implications of ending the tax deductions mentioned below, which is essentially a tax increase on the oil and gas industry resulting in a reduction in domestic energy production, which would result in an increase of oil from overseas suppliers. That said, in regard to tax policy, I believe that all industries should be treated the same, irrespective of the product that the industry produces.

There are those who complain about the earnings of the oil and gas companies without understanding the nature of the business, which is the most capital-intensive in the world. The oil and natural gas industry must make large investments in new technology, new production, and environmental and product quality improvements to meet future U.S. energy needs. These investments are not only in the oil and gas sector but in alternate forms of energy (e.g., biofuels). For example, an Ernst & Young study shows the five major oil companies had $765 billion of new investment between 1992 and 2006, compared to net income of $662 billion during the same period. The 57 largest U.S. oil and natural gas companies had new investments of $1.25 trillion over the same period, compared to net income of $900 billion and cash flows of $1.77 trillion. In another Ernst and Young report, the 50 largest oil and gas companies spent over $106 billion in exploration and development costs in 2011, an increase of 38 percent over those capital investments in 2010. Without these investments, the U.S. oil and gas industry would not have been able to make the strides in increased oil and gas production that they have made and continue to make in this country.[1] Earnings allow companies to reinvest in facilities, infrastructure and new technologies, and when those investments are in the United States, it means many more jobs, directly and indirectly. It also means more revenues for federal, state and local governments.

Question. Ukraine's reliance on Russian natural gas to meet half of its domestic needs has left it vulnerable to predatory Russian practices in terms of energy supply manipulation. Yet Ukraine has vast untapped domestic natural gas supplies and it is also the second-least energy efficient country in the world. I have introduced legislation—S. 2433—that aims to double U.S. Government-wide energy assistance to Ukraine to help them increase efficiency, develop their own resources, and get off Russian gas.

◆ Do you support this legislation? Please provide any thoughts or technical feedback about this legislation.

Answer. For years, the United States experienced declining natural gas production and was constructing terminals for liquefied natural gas (LNG) imports to ensure that the United States had an adequate supply of natural gas in the future. The reason the United States now produces the most natural gas in the world and no longer needs to rely on LNG imports is not because of government programs, but because of technological improvements in the market place, private property rights, and prudent regulations by state regulators. Policymakers should promote these proven avenues that have led to natural gas energy independence and growing market power for the United States. If Senator Markey believes that Ukraine is vulnerable to hostile governments because it has not fully tapped its domestic gas supplies, Senator Markey should agree that the U.S. Government should not commit a similar mistake by hampering the development of American oil and gas supplies, as the Obama administration is currently doing.

If it is the case that Ukrainian Government is hampering the development of its own domestic gas resources, then Ukrainian people would be served by eliminating such obstacles. However, the U.S. Government does not need to assist Ukrainian Government in implementing a policy that makes Ukrainians wealthier and more strategically secure. Furthermore, S. 2433 contains provisions for the U.S. Government to provide ''loan, lease, and bond guarantees'' to financial institutions to facilitate the goals of the proposed legislation.[2] Such guarantees place U.S. taxpayers on the hook in the event of a default. There is no economic rationale for U.S. taxpayers to effectively subsidize Ukrainians to do what it is in their own best interest.

Question. You made your critical views on the Cape Wind offshore wind project, and government support for it, very clear during the hearing. What are your views on the $8.3 billion loan guarantee, most of which has been finalized, to construct nuclear reactors?

Answer. The Energy Information Administration (EIA) estimates the levelized cost of new generating technologies as part of its Annual Energy Outlook. The average cost of offshore wind in the agency's 2014 outlook is 20.4 cents per kilowatt hour while the levelized cost for advanced nuclear is 9.6 cents per kilowatt hour, or less than half the cost of offshore wind.[3] Given that EIA also expects advanced nuclear to have a 90-percent capacity factor while offshore wind has only a 37-percent capacity factor on average, the amount of generation from nuclear power compared to wind power would be 2.4 times more for the same amount of generating capacity. Further, wind is an intermittent technology and cannot be relied on continuously to supply power when Americans need it most. It generates power only when the wind blows which is more prevalent at night when we need it the least. Because Cape Wind will drive up the cost of energy for Americans based on its contract specifications, I do not support it.

Compared to offshore wind, which is an intermittent, inefficient, and expensive technology, nuclear power is reliable, efficient, and more affordable as the numbers from EIA above demonstrate.

That said, I believe it is a bad idea for taxpayers to support either technology (or any technology for that matter). The Federal Government has demonstrated time and time again with companies like Solyndra that it is ill-suited to pick winners in the marketplace. The reason that the government supports specific technologies is the belief that consumers will not willingly pay for those technologies. When elected officials impose their choice of technologies on consumers and taxpayers, other technologies that could have made it in the marketplace on their own are locked out—and the consumers who would have preferred those technologies—suffer.

Question. Thanks to an oil company court challenge to a 1995 law, oil companies are able to drill on many leases in the Gulf of Mexico without paying any royalties to the American taxpayers. Currently, oil companies are paying zero royalties to taxpayers for one-quarter of all offshore oil production in the United States. Incentivizing companies to renegotiate these leases in order to pay a fair return to the public could save taxpayers $15.5 billion over 10 years according to the Department of the Interior. The Government Accountability Office has estimated that taxpayers could lose up to $53 billion over the life of these faulty leases.

◆ Would you support legislation to correct this problem, which the Congressional Research Service has found is within Congress' legal authority and would not abrogate contracts between oil companies and the Federal Government?

Answer. I am grateful for the opportunity to set the record straight on the deep-water royalty relief program. Oil is being produced in the deep water Federal Gulf of Mexico, where production just increased during fiscal year 2013 for the first time since the moratorium on drilling was imposed by the Obama administration in 2010, because of the royalty relief program. The program originally provided royalty relief for operators to develop fields in water depths greater than 200 meters (656 feet). The suspension of Federal royalty payments for new leases was limited to a certain level of production based on water depth. The original terms and conditions expired in November 2000, and since that time, a revised incentive plan was adopted that is no longer based on volumes determined by water-depth intervals. Instead, the Department of Interior assigns a lease-specific volume of royalty suspension based on how the determined suspension amount may affect the economics of various development scenarios with the most economically risky projects receiving the most relief, while others may receive no relief. For example, a deep-water field might not receive any relief if it is adjacent to an existing gathering system. On the other hand, a similar field may receive a great deal of relief if it is located far beyond the current pipeline infrastructure.[4]

If the royalty relief program did not exist, the technology would not have been developed to produce oil and natural gas in the deep water Gulf of Mexico and domestic oil production would be much lower—clearly reducing America's energy security and making the United States more dependent on foreign imports. This is consistent with the points made by the Honorable Hazel O'Leary, Secretary of Energy during the Clinton administration.

In a letter on page H11872 of the Congressional Record in support of the legislation at the time,[5] the Secretary said, "Comparing this loss (foregone royalties) with the gain from the bonus bids on a net present value basis, the Federal Government would be ahead by $200 million. It is important to note that affected OCS projects would still pay a substantial upfront bonus and then be required to pay a royalty when and if production exceeds their royalty-free period. A royalty-free period, such as that proposed in S. 395, would help enable marginally viable OCS projects to be developed, thus providing additional energy, jobs and other important benefits to the nation."

On the matter of national security, she went on to add, "The ability to lower costs of domestic production in the central and western Gulf of Mexico by providing appropriate fiscal incentives will lead to an expansion of domestic energy resources, enhance national energy security, and reduce the deficit."

Clearly, President Clinton and his administration studied this matter and saw it as a significant national security benefit to the United States, and a benefit, not a loss, to the U.S. Treasury. Besides providing the American public with more oil and gas production and greater energy security, thousands of jobs exist today because of the royalty relief program.

Question. Last-In, First-Out (LIFO) accounting allows oil companies to value their inventories at deeply discounted prices. Repealing this subsidy for the largest oil and gas companies would generate at least $14.1 billion over 10 years, according to the Joint Committee on Taxation (JCT).

◆ Is there any other industry that benefits from this tax subsidy as much as the oil and gas sector? If so, which sector(s) and how much do they benefit from this subsidy? Would you support ending this accounting methodology for all taxpayers?

Answer. All U.S. taxpayers may use the LIFO (Last-In-First-Out) method of accounting for inventories. Repealing this provision for just the oil and gas industry would be particularly detrimental to refiners, who maintain large inventories of both crude and refined products. I believe that all industries should be treated the same under the U.S. tax law and that one industry should not be singled out for differential treatment. This accounting methodology should either be allowed for all taxpayers or repealed for all taxpayers.

Question. Foreign tax credits allow all companies that do business abroad to reduce from their U.S. tax bill by any income taxes paid to other governments. However, these rules were not intended to allow oil companies to claim deductions for what amount to royalty payments to foreign governments. Such payments are not income taxes but fees for the privilege of producing valuable natural resources abroad. Yet, as a result of loosely drafted rules, oil companies are frequently deducting these payments from their U.S. tax liability. Eliminating this tax treatment for the largest oil companies would generate at least $6.5 billion over 10 years, according to the JCT.

  ◆ Would you support ending this tax subsidy for the largest oil companies? Is there any other industry that benefits from this tax subsidy as much as the oil and gas sector? If so, which sector(s) and how much do they benefit from this provision?

Answer. The above issue relates to dual capacity rules and according to the Joint Committee on Taxation, U.S. oil and gas companies are already limited in their ability to claim these credits.[6] Further, the purported issue that you describe; i.e., that companies claim royalty payments as a foreign tax credit, is prevented by the current rules for this provision. Oil and gas companies are under constant audit by the Internal Revenue Service. As a part of these audits, teams of examiners focus heavily on this very issue. If an IRS agent feels that there is an issue related to mischaracterization of a tax payment, he or she need not "prove" the case, but merely needs to raise the question. The taxpayer is then required, under the law, to prove that the payment was, in fact, a payment of tax and not a royalty, and to provide that proof in court, if necessary. The burden of proof rests heavily on the taxpayer in this instance. Modifications to this provision will make U.S. companies less competitive and place a greater share of oil and gas reserves into the hands of non-U.S. companies, employing non-U.S. workers; many of which are foreign-government-controlled.

Question. The section 199 domestic manufacturing deduction was enacted in 2004 and recategorized the oil industry as a manufacturing industry, thus making it eligible for this deduction. Repealing this provision for the largest oil companies would save $10.4 billion over the next 10 years, according to the JCT.

  ◆ Would you support ending this tax subsidy for the largest oil companies?

Answer. The purpose of the domestic manufacturing tax deduction is to incentivize companies to continue to do business in America. The United States now has the highest tax rate in the world among developed countries, and due to these high tax rates, companies have been making investments overseas.[7] The domestic manufacturing tax deduction allows all industries and businesses (not just oil companies) to deduct a certain percentage of their profits. For the oil and gas industry, the tax deduction is 6 percent; for all other industries (software developers, video game developers, the motion picture industry, among others), it is a 9-percent deduction.[8] Removing these tax deductions will result in oil companies taking capital abroad to make their investments, reducing U.S. oil production and tax revenues and increasing imports of foreign oil. Given that oil and gas production-related employment on non-Federal lands in the United States is one of the few bright spots in the worst economic recovery since the Great Depression, such a result would undermine job creation.

Question. The expensing of intangible drilling costs allows intangible drilling costs, such as wages, repairs, and supplies related to and necessary for drilling and preparing wells for the production of oil and gas, to be deducted in the year they occurred. Nonenergy companies must depreciate these costs over time. The JCT estimates that repealing this subsidy will generate $13.2 billion over 10 years.

  ◆ Are any other companies besides oil and gas production companies eligible for claiming this tax provision? Would you support ending this tax subsidy?

Answer. This incentive exists to encourage small companies (less than 20 employees) to produce oil from marginal wells that are old or small and do not produce much oil individually. According to the Independent Petroleum Association of America, independent producers drill 95 percent of the oil and natural gas wells in America, producing 54 percent of U.S. liquids—54 percent oil and 81 percent condensates. They reinvest 150 percent of their American cash flow back into new American production.[9]

Independent oil producers are allowed to count certain costs associated with the drilling and development of these wells as business expenses. This ability to expense these costs is analogous to the research and development (R&D) deduction available to all taxpayers engaged in R&D activities. The law allows the small producers to expense the full value of these costs, known as intangible drilling costs, every year to encourage them to explore for new oil. The major companies get a portion of this deduction—they can expense a third of intangible drilling costs, but they must spread the deductions across a 5-year period.[10]

Again, I believe that all industries should be treated the same under the tax law and that one industry should not be singled out for differential treatment because the terminology used is different.

Question. Certain oil companies amortize the costs of exploratory work in 2 years, while other companies must amortize those same costs over 7 years. Increasing geological and geophysical amortization periods for oil and gas companies to 7 years would harmonize this policy across industries and operators. The JCT estimates that making this change would save taxpayers as much as $1.1 billion over 10 years. Would you support this change in tax policy to eliminate a subsidy?

Answer. Independent producers and smaller integrated companies are currently allowed to amortize geological and geophysical (G&G) costs over a 2-year period, whereas major integrated producers may only amortize over 7 years.[11] According to the Joint Committee on Taxation, G&G costs are costs incurred for the purpose of obtaining and accumulating data that will serve as acquisition and retention of mineral properties,[12] which are akin to research and development expenses that most companies can expense in one year.

"Research and development, or R&D, are the lifeblood of technological advancement, and they factor heavily in most corporate enterprises' planning and growth. Recognizing the importance of technology and business growth in the international marketplace, the U.S. Congress created tax breaks for companies that engage in R&D. As an incentive to engage in research and development, the IRS permits businesses to deduct all R&D expenses in a single year instead of amortizing as a capital expense."[13]

Again, I believe that all industries should be treated the same under the tax law and that one industry should not be singled out for differential treatment because the terminology used is different.

Question. Oil and gas properties qualify for "percentage depletion," a tax deduction of 15 percent of gross revenues from the well, even if the deductions exceed the well's value over time. The JCT estimates that repealing this provision for the large oil companies would generate $11.9 billion over 10 years.

◆ Do you support the repeal of this tax subsidy? Are any other companies besides oil and gas production companies eligible for claiming this tax subsidy?

Answer. I am grateful for the opportunity to set the record straight on the percentage depletion tax deduction that the small independent oil producers are allowed to deduct on their taxes. As the oil and gas in a well is depleted, the small independent producers are allowed a percentage depletion allowance to be deducted from their taxes. While the percentage depletion allowance sounds complicated, it is similar to the treatment given other businesses for depreciation of an asset. The tax code essentially treats the value of a well as it does the value of a newly constructed factory, allowing a percentage of the value to be depreciated each year. This allowance was first instituted in 1926 to compensate for the decreasing value of the resource, and was eliminated for major oil companies in 1975.[14] This allowance applies only to the first 1,000 barrels of production during the period, so it is of little significance to large independent producers. It saves the independent oil and gas producers about $1 billion in taxes per year.[15] It is true that repealing this provision would extract more tax revenue from these energy producers since that is what tax hikes do, but it would make sense from neither an economic nor accounting perspective. When oil is removed from a well and sold, the remaining value of the well does go down. The percentage depletion deduction addresses this reality of oil and gas production.

Question. Under the tax rules governing tertiary injectants, oil companies deduct expenses relating to the cost of tertiary injectants during the taxable year, instead of depreciating these costs over a typical cost recovery schedule. Ending this subsidy for large oil companies would generate $32 million over 10 years, according to the JCT.

◆ Do you support the repeal of this tax subsidy? Are any other companies besides oil and gas production companies eligible for claiming this tax subsidy?

Answer. According to the Joint Committee on Taxation, oil and gas companies can deduct tertiary injectant expenses during the taxable year,[16] similar to a business expense of other companies. This provision was provided to the oil and gas industry to increase domestic oil production, providing greater energy security for the nation. And, it is continuing to be effective. For example, domestic oil production from enhanced oil recovery is expected to increase in EIA's Annual Energy Outlook projections by over 160 percent between 2012 and 2040,[17] which shows that this tax provision is fulfilling its intended purpose of increasing domestic oil production, thereby increasing energy security.

Question. Taxpayers can shelter active income through passive losses or credits associated with the production of oil and gas, a condition that does not apply to other sources of passive income or credit. Repealing the exception for passive loss limitations for oil and gas properties for oil companies with revenues above $50 million per year would generate $9 million over 10 years, according to the JCT.

◆ Would you support this change to harmonize tax treatment so as not to favor oil and gas investments over other types of energy investments?

Answer. Although this is not a specifically energy-related topic, in the spirit of promoting economic efficiency and avoiding the government picking winners and losers, IER supports broad-based tax reform that would eliminate all tax credits and deductions for all firms, so long as marginal tax rates were reduced across-the-board to maintain revenue neutrality. This reform would flatten the tax code and consistently apply the same rules to everybody, removing the temptation for government officials to dole out privileges to favored groups by partially shielding them from the full burden of the code. IER would fully support Senator Markey if he chooses to promote such broad-based tax reform. However, if Senator Markey believes it is good policy to discriminate against a particular industry merely because they produce hydrocarbons, then Senator Markey's proposal will not provide efficient tax reform but instead will simply be a tax hike on one of the few sectors of our economy that has been consistently producing jobs since the recession began.

End Notes

[1] Ernst and Young, U.S. E&P Benchmark Study, June 2012.
[2] https://beta.congress.gov/bill/113th-congress/senate-bill/2433.
[3] Energy Information Administration, Levelized Cost and Levelized Avoided Cost of New Generation Resources in the Annual Energy Outlook 2014, April 17, 2014.
[4] Encyclopedia of Earth, Deep Water Royalty Relief Act, July 17, 2011.
[5] Congressional Record, November 8, 1995.
[6] Joint Committee on Taxation, Description of Present Law and Select Proposals Relating to the Oil and Gas Industry, May 12, 2011.
[7] US News, World's Highest Corporate Tax Rate Hurts U.S. Economically, April 2, 2012.
[8] Scientific American, End Oil Subsidies? The $4 Billion Dollar Question, February 21, 2012.
[9] Independent Petroleum Association of America.
[10] Trib.com, Obama tax changes could hit small oil and gas operators in Wyoming, March 30, 2012.
[11] Joint Committee on Taxation, Description of Present Law and Select Proposals Relating to the Oil and Gas Industry, May 12, 2011.
[12] Joint Committee on Taxation, Description of Present Law and Select Proposals Relating to the Oil and Gas Industry, May 12, 2011.
[13] Small Business, Tax Breaks for R&D.
[14] Star Tribune, Obama tax changes could hit small oil and gas operators in Wyoming, March 30, 2012.
[15] Scientific American, End Oil Subsidies? The $4 Billion Dollar Question, February 21, 2012.
[16] Joint Committee on Taxation, Description of Present Law and Select Proposals Relating to the Oil and Gas Industry, May 12, 2011.
[17] Energy Information Administration, Annual Energy Outlook 2014.

RESPONSE OF MICHAEL BREEN TO QUESTION
SUBMITTED BY SENATOR EDWARD J. MARKEY

Question. Ukraine's reliance on Russian natural gas to meet half of its domestic needs has left it vulnerable to predatory Russian practices in terms of energy supply manipulation. Yet Ukraine has vast untapped domestic natural gas supplies and it is also the second-least energy efficient country in the world. I have introduced legislation—S. 2433—that aims to double U.S. government-wide energy assistance to Ukraine to help them increase efficiency, develop their own resources, and get off Russian gas.

◆ Do you support this legislation? Please provide any thoughts or technical feedback about this legislation.

Answer. I strongly support S. 2433, which offers an important and viable path forward for Ukraine's energy security. As Chairman Markey noted, Ukraine is heavily reliant on Russian natural gas to meet its energy needs, importing more than 60 percent of its natural gas consumption in 2013 from Russia. Russia has consistently exploited Ukraine's energy reliance for geopolitical gains, most recently cutting off exports completely since June. Ukraine also uses far more energy than it should. Outmoded district heating networks, poorly insulated housing, leaky pipes, and ancient boilers all exacerbate Ukraine's need for energy, which makes the country more vulnerable.

S. 2433 properly applies efficiency as a tool to help Ukraine achieve energy security. By ensuring that energy efficiency improvements are a priority of U.S. Government and international aid to Ukraine, S. 2433 will deliver the most certain reductions in Moscow's geopolitical leverage over Kiev. Additionally, by helping Ukraine develop its own energy sources, including renewable sources, S. 2433 will help assuage concerns of a looming gas crisis in the European Union, as Ukraine serves as an important transit hub for natural gas.

Most importantly, S. 2433 serves as a model for U.S. energy diplomacy in the future. America's greatest strength has always been technological innovation and technical knowledge. We should prioritize those assets in our foreign policy. By maximizing Ukraine's ability to provide for its own energy future, we will help minimize the vulnerabilities of our allies and the geopolitical leverage of our adversaries.

————

RESPONSES OF ERIC POSTEL TO QUESTIONS
SUBMITTED BY SENATOR EDWARD J. MARKEY

Question. Does your agency have the information and resources needed to understand and integrate the impacts of climate change on its mission? If not, what is needed?

Answer. Integrating climate change in Agency programming, policy dialogue, and operations is one of three strategic objectives in USAID's Climate Change and Development Strategy, with the other two being mitigation and adaptation.

Staff dedicated to helping USAID understand and integrate the impacts of climate change are assigned not only to the Bureau for Economic Growth, Education, and Environment, but also to the Bureau for Food Security, Bureau for Democracy, Conflict and Humanitarian Assistance, and the Africa, Latin America and Caribbean, and Asia Bureaus. These climate-change specialists lend their knowledge of, and experience in, climate change to inform key Agency programs and policy discussions.

All USAID missions are required to fully consider climate change as they develop their Country Development and Cooperation Strategies. Supplemental guidance for climate-related programming provides missions with technical guidance on how they can best incorporate climate change into country strategies. In addition, climate-change specialists review and comment on draft strategy documents and, thus far, have provided significant support to nine missions with their strategies. More than half of final mission strategies substantially incorporate climate change.

USAID is also working to bring climate change into sharper focus through the environmental compliance process—an entry point to promote project design that considers and integrates climate change. USAID policy includes ''identify[ing] impacts resulting from AID's actions upon the environment'' and ''defin[ing] environmental limiting factors that constrain development.'' This provides ample scope not only to avoid greenhouse gas emissions and maladaptation, but also to address climate change impacts as potential limiting factors on USAID's development work. A climate change module has been included in environmental compliance trainings for USAID staff and implementers, and information on climate change has been added to USAID's Sector Environmental Guidelines, a resource that helps compliance officers, project designers, and implementers think through environmental compliance in specific sectors.

USAID's recently released Climate Resilient Development Framework provides guidance to USAID staff, implementers, and others on how to consider and address climate change impacts in development work. The Agency intranet and other relevant platforms, such as the Feed the Future knowledge management portal, AgriLinks, make this and other resources available to staff at their fingertips.

Training is also an important element of USAID's climate change integration strategy. To date, we have trained more than 500 USAID employees on how to take climate change impacts into account and design projects that contribute to climate change adaptation, or on how to address climate change in specific sectors, such as agriculture, infrastructure, and water. Trainings take place in Washington and in high-priority missions.

USAID is also expanding its knowledge of the impacts of climate change integration through monitoring and evaluating climate change integration projects. A series of performance and impact evaluations are underway.

Finally, policy determinations such as Executive Order 13653 issued on November 1, 2013, to strengthen coordinated action on climate change preparedness and resilience across the Federal Government, give impetus to the Agency to strengthen and build on efforts in climate change. USAID is revising its Agency Adaptation Plan in response to Executive Order 13653 and implementation of the prioritized actions listed in that plan will further enhance the integration of climate change impacts into the Agency's work.

Question. What are the impacts of hydrocarbon price volatility in the developing world?

Answer. The main impacts of hydrocarbon price volatility in the developing world depend on whether a country is a hydrocarbon importer or exporter.

Importers

For hydrocarbon importing countries, volatility of hydrocarbon import prices can drive a number of outcomes. For example, hydrocarbon imports, and increases in hydrocarbon prices, tend to put pressure on current account balances and drive depreciation of local currencies. Net importers, such as India, Kenya, and recently Egypt and Pakistan, face growing import bills for their coal, oil, and gas imports.

In many cases, the problem is a combination of increasing hydrocarbon prices and energy subsidization that puts serious financial strain on government budgets in developing countries. Energy subsidies often crowd out public expenditures on health, education, and infrastructure. For example, Egypt's fuel subsidies now consume almost 25 percent of the government's budget. In 2011, a review found energy subsidies were more than three times the spending by the central government on education, and seven times health expenditures.[1] Additionally, USAID reviewed Pakistan's budget in 2009 and found fuel subsidies were five times the central government's expenditure on health and education.

As energy subsidy costs grow, many governments have tried to reduce the subsidy burden by raising domestic fuel and electricity prices. Reducing hydrocarbon subsidies—and raising prices to accommodate rising hydrocarbon prices—is frequently associated with civil disorder. Bolivia, Bulgaria, Guinea, Indonesia, Jordan, Mozambique, Nigeria, Pakistan, Tunisia, to name some recent examples, have had riots over energy costs. In 2013, the Bulgarian Government fell due to public objections to energy price increases.

Exporters

One of the main effects of hydrocarbon price volatility on hydrocarbon exporting countries is budgetary shortfalls when prices decline. Many countries rely heavily on hydrocarbon revenues as both a source of government revenues and foreign exchange earnings. For example, Nigeria's Government relies on hydrocarbon exports for 75 percent of its budget[2] and over 95 percent of the country's foreign exchange earnings.[3] Changes in global oil prices therefore have a major impact on Nigeria's public finances.

USAID works in a number of countries that have recently begun to develop significant new hydrocarbon resource finds, including Ghana, Tanzania, South Sudan, and Uganda. These countries will have to cope with the variability of global export prices when managing their resource revenues and budgets. Nonoil related industry can be hurt by the resulting volatile, and often high, foreign exchange rates.

Another serious challenge is effective hydrocarbon sector governance and avoiding mismanagement of both environmental impacts and public revenues.

Question. How does USAID evaluate the best way to help partner countries overcome these challenges?

Answer. USAID takes a strategic approach to providing energy sector assistance. This approach must balance multiple objectives of the U.S. Government in its relationship with developing countries. Objectives that are considered include:

• Energy security and energy for sustainable economic growth.

---

[1] Energy Subsidies in the Middle East and North Africa: Lessons for Reform, International Monetary Fund, March 2014.
[2] Forbes, 7 April 2014.
[3] Michigan State University Broad School of Business Global Edge service.

- Mitigating climate change through low emissions development planning and clean energy development.
- Increasing energy access for poverty reduction.
- Energy sector reconstruction in conflict and post-disaster countries.

For countries that are hydrocarbon importers, USAID programs focus on activities such as improving energy efficiency, scaling up renewable energy, and developing domestic energy resources. Afghanistan and Pakistan are good examples where USAID is helping to promote renewable energy, including hydroelectric generation. In addition, we have supported the development of local gas production by working closely with the World Bank, Asian Development Bank, and Afghan Government to develop the large gas fields in northern Afghanistan, near the border with Turkmenistan.

USAID also views improved performance of energy service providers—public utilities—as an important part of the solution. Helping public utilities perform better makes it easier for countries to cope with fuel price volatility. As losses go down, utilities generally become financially stronger, more capable of keeping up with fuel payments, and are better able to invest in both renewable energy and other low cost generation sources.

We work with many countries with utility systems that have very low cost recovery and high losses in the electricity sector. USAID supports utility performance improvement programs in a number of countries, including Afghanistan, Ghana, India, Kosovo, Pakistan, South Sudan, and Tanzania.

For countries with high levels of energy subsidies, subsidy reform can have big payoffs in terms of higher growth and greater equity; yet, energy subsidy reform is complex, both technically and politically. USAID has found that careful planning, including on the timing and pace of reform is essential. Likewise, consideration of social safety nets along with a public information campaign that raises awareness about the subsidy costs and benefits of reform are needed.

Recent developments in the pricing of on-shore wind and solar photovoltaic generation also have an impact on countries' ability to cope with high fuel bills. In the past several years, these two renewable options have begun to reach price parity with hydrocarbon-based generation, although this varies by country. As an example, wind energy in some Indian states is cheaper than electricity generated by a new plant using imported coal. In India, solar plants are currently being bid by private developers at rates that are lower than generation plants using imported liquefied natural gas or diesel fuel.

Some countries that rely heavily on imported fuel for generation are finding it cost effective to introduce wind and solar power into their systems, including Indonesia, the Philippines, and many Caribbean and South Pacific Islands.

Similarly, solar power prices in some of the countries where USAID works, including Brazil, India, Mexico, Nigeria and South Africa are comparable to the consumer retail electricity rate. When renewables reach parity with hydrocarbon-based generation, countries can invest in renewable generation as a means of coping with high fuel costs.

In hydrocarbon-exporting countries, challenges are often associated with sector governance, protection of public revenues, and environmental impacts. USAID evaluates the strategic role that hydrocarbon exports play in a country's development, but it does not have large assistance programs related to hydrocarbon sector development. In recent years, assistance related to hydrocarbon exports has been provided by other U.S. Government agencies, such as the Department of State's Energy and Natural Resources Bureau.

Question. Please provide us with your views of the hot spots you are especially concerned about in terms of the potential for climate change impacts to generate major destabilization in the future. As you're looking at the people living closest to the edge, where day-to-day survival can be a struggle, where could a catastrophic drought or storm or flood or other climate change-related extreme weather event put communities or regions over the edge?

Answer. USAID has conducted analysis and applied research on these issues from a development perspective since 2008. While the science and practice of analyzing the interaction of climate change risk and conflict risk is still evolving, we do have some topline findings in which we have high confidence. First, as the Intergovernmental Panel on Climate Change's Fifth Assessment Report finds, the presence of violent conflict strongly influences vulnerability to climate change impacts for people living in affected places. Therefore, we need to prioritize attention to conflict prevention and peace-building as a complement to climate adaptation efforts in those places.

Conversely, there is an increasing body of evidence suggesting that climate impacts are a threat multiplier that significantly increases the potential for conflict in places with already weak institutional and social capacity to respond. A majority of the world's most fragile regions, countries, and communities—where conflict and violence is most likely and persistent—also will likely be highly exposed to the impacts of climate change. For example, in Africa, Asia, and Latin America we already see competition and conflict over issues such as deforestation and access to arable land. Water shortages are one of the most immediate pressing threats to lives and livelihoods in water-stressed areas such as the Middle East, North Africa and the Horn of Africa, but we also see potential impacts in regions dependent on glaciers for water—including Asia and the Andean region.

Conflict is certainly not a foregone conclusion when climatic stresses are added to these scenarios of vulnerability, but when those additional stresses are not met with established approaches to increase resilience and managed by effective institutional responses, then the likelihood of violence as a strategy to resolve grievances increases.

Question. Is this sort of ongoing strategic examination part of your Bureau or how is it institutionalized at USAID?

Answer. USAID's Office of Conflict Management and Mitigation within the Bureau for Democracy, Conflict and Humanitarian Assistance develops and disseminates rigorous field-relevant research, analysis, and guidance to better understand conflict dynamics based on a comprehensive knowledge management system. That office has also been leading the Agency's efforts to understand and respond to the risks associated with climate change impacts in fragile states, including cutting-edge research to guide conflict-sensitive climate adaptation and resilience approaches globally.

Question. Ukraine's reliance on Russian natural gas to meet half of its domestic needs has left it vulnerable to predatory Russian practices in terms of energy supply manipulation. Yet Ukraine has vast untapped domestic natural gas supplies and it is also the second-least energy efficient country in the world. I have introduced legislation—S. 2433—that aims to double U.S. Government-wide energy assistance to Ukraine to help them increase efficiency, develop their own resources, and get off Russian gas.

◆ Do you support this legislation? Please provide any thoughts or technical feedback about this legislation.

Answer. USAID agrees that Ukraine needs to increase energy efficiency and supply diversity for a more secure and resilient energy sector. The legislation describes several activities that, if well implemented and coordinated, could assist Ukraine in becoming more energy independent and energy efficient. To that end, USAID engages key stakeholders throughout Ukraine's energy sector and the donor community to modernize energy infrastructure, improve energy sector governance, and support the integration of Ukraine into the European Union.

In Ukraine, USAID supports participation in high-level and technical working groups on crucial issues such as providing social safety nets in the face of rising tariffs, supporting municipal heating improvement and energy efficiency, and reforming tariffs to reflect appropriate cost of service. This initiative builds on past efforts that leveraged $225 million for energy efficiency projects, leading to savings of 380 million cubic meters of natural gas.

USAID also continues to assist the National Electricity Regulatory Commission of Ukraine in building its capacity to oversee a market-based energy sector, including support for developing a regulatory framework harmonized with European Union directives and moving toward cost-reflective tariffs necessary to encourage energy efficiency. Ukraine's transmission system operator participates in a USAID-led regional working group that identifies necessary infrastructure investments for improving cross-border electricity trade. In addition, USAID is fulfilling a pledge of $7.5 million to a ÷90 million Eastern Europe partnership fund that supports energy efficiency in public infrastructure in Ukraine and has funded several prior assessments to help Ukraine identify pathways to alternative energy sources.

Given the scale of the energy challenge facing Ukraine, USAID would use any additional resources to leverage its current work and relationships within the country to increase Ukraine's energy security.

RESPONSES OF AMOS HOCHSTEIN TO QUESTIONS
SUBMITTED BY SENATOR JOHN BARRASSO

Question. What is the total number of staff positions at the Bureau of Energy Resources?

Answer. ENR has 65 authorized full-time equivalent (FTE) positions. In addition, the Bureau employs a number of nonpermanent staff and fellows.

Question. What is the fiscal year 2013 and 2014 budget for the Bureau of Energy Resources?

Answer. The total FY 2013 Bureau of Energy Resources budget was $21,613,245. The total FY 2014 budget was $23,683,000. This represents an increase of $2,069,755.

Question. What percentage of the work done by the Bureau of Energy Resources involves international climate change projects?

Answer. The Bureau of Energy Resources (ENR) focuses on energy resources including oil, gas, nuclear, coal and renewable energy integration. In the Department of State, the Office of the Special Envoy for Climate Change (S/SECC) represents the United States internationally at the ministerial level in all bilateral and multilateral negotiations regarding climate change. The Bureau of Oceans and International Environmental and Scientific Affairs (OES) handles all environment and climate programs in support of S/SECC.

Question. Is international climate change a top priority of the Bureau of Energy Resources?

Answer. The Bureau of Energy Resources is focused on issues that affect the security, economic competitiveness, and environmental sustainability of world energy supplies and markets. ENR unites U.S. diplomatic and programmatic efforts to build sustainable, transparent, and predictable international markets for oil, natural gas, coal, civil nuclear power, electricity, renewable energy, and energy efficiency that advance U.S. national security interests and a strong national and global economy.

Question. Global Climate Change Programs.—The Global Climate Change Initiative seeks to integrate climate change considerations into foreign assistance programs. The fiscal year 2015 budget requests $506.3 million for global climate change related activities supported by State and USAID, a 10-percent increase over the fiscal year 2013 level.

◆ Given the increasing need for humanitarian assistance, democracy promotion, and embassy security measures, why is $506.3 million for global climate change the best expenditure of taxpayer funds?
◆ Since 2010, how much funding has the U.S. Department of State spent on international climate change programs?

Most aid programs are not evaluated to determine the actual impact of the assistance. Congress as well as the American people cannot determine whether taxpayer dollars are being used wisely when it is unclear if it succeeded or failed.

◆ What percentage of State's international climate change programs have completed evaluations?
◆ Have those evaluations been made available to Congress and the public? Where can they be accessed?
◆ What is the timeline for the completion of all of the reviews assessing whether the international climate change projects are meeting their goals and are having the intended impact?

Answer.

Æ The objective of the President's Global Climate Change Initiative (GCCI) is to help countries grow their economies in a way that reduces carbon pollution, builds their resilience to climate impacts and disasters, and mobilizes investment for the climate and clean energy solutions of the future.

Climate change is projected to have major impacts on weather-sensitive economic sectors and water supply abroad, with especially adverse effects on poor and vulnerable countries, impacting their ability to develop and achieve prosperity. Extreme weather events such as drought, floods, and storms aggravate problems such as poverty, social tensions, and environmental degradation that reduce prospects for prosperity and undermine development. The Council of Economic Advisers estimates that warming of 3 degrees Celsius above preindustrial levels, instead of 2 degrees Celsius, could increase annual economic damages by approximately 0.9 percent of global output. To put this percentage in perspective for the United States, 0.9 percent of estimated 2014 U.S. GDP is approximately $150 billion, and the incremental costs beyond 3 degrees Celsius would be even greater. The Department of Defense and independent defense assessments have identified climate change as a threat multiplier in vulnerable parts of the world, with significant national security risks for the United States.

Successfully combating climate change will require decisive global action. It is strongly in the U.S. interest that fast-growing developing countries do their part to stem their emissions, even as we work to do the same. This initiative request comes at a pivotal moment. The actions countries commit to taking this year will be a major determinant of the trajectory of GHG emissions and associated climate change that will occur in coming decades, and the strength of those actions will consequently have a significant bearing on the severity of anticipated climate impacts both in the United States and abroad.

The GCCI is essential in leveraging effective GHG reduction efforts from developing countries. It helps countries undertake climate mitigation efforts, and it will help us ensure through global negotiations that developing countries do their part. These investments ensure that the United States is a leader in helping vulnerable countries cope with the impacts of climate change, and in helping to put the globe on a path toward development that is cleaner and more efficient.

GCCI programs not only benefit our efforts to protect our climate system, they promote our broader development objectives. Virtually all GCCI programs have important benefits for food security, health, sustainability, economic development and poverty reduction, and regional stability, all of which benefit the U.S. and global economy.

Æ The Department of State has dedicated $712.2 million to international climate change programs with funds appropriated in FY 2010 through FY 2014.

Æ The Department continually monitors and evaluates GCCI activities in compliance with Department evaluation policies. Prior to the January 2015 evaluation policy update, the Department required that all large programs or projects be evaluated at least once in their lifetime or every 5 years, whichever was less. The Department actively monitors all programs, including those administered through multilateral mechanisms that we support, and multilateral programs and funding routinely undergo independent audit and evaluation.

Æ A majority of State GCCI programming has undergone or is currently undergoing performance monitoring and evaluation or assessment. For example, the Asia Pacific Partnership on Clean Development and Climate (APP) evaluation reviewed the APP model including the leadership, administration, and resources of this public-private partnership from 2007–2009. Similarly, an ongoing, 3-year evaluation of the GCCI, will assess the data quality of reported outcomes for all State-funded GCCI projects. Other evaluations, such as the completed Global Methane Initiative evaluation, and the ongoing Climate Renewables and Deployment Initiative (Climate REDI) evaluation, focus on large, substantive GCCI programs.

Æ Beginning in 2015, summaries of all evaluations performed with foreign assistance funds can be found at www.state.gov/f/evaluations/index.htm. USAID evaluations are also publicly available on the Development Experience Clearinghouse Web site: https://dec.usaid.gov/dec/home/Default.aspx.

Æ Evaluations are ongoing and the design and procurement of new evaluations occurs annually. Additionally, project implementers provide semi-annual reporting that includes performance results across standard GCCI indicators to allow leadership to reflect upon progress toward meeting GCCI goals. These results are reported annually and cumulatively through the Department's Performance Plan and Report and a subset is publicly reported on through the Annual Performance Plan and Report.

RESPONSES OF ERIC POSTEL TO QUESTIONS
SUBMITTED BY SENATOR JOHN BARRASSO

GLOBAL CLIMATE CHANGE PROGRAMS

The Global Climate Change Initiative seeks to integrate climate change considerations into foreign assistance programs. The fiscal year 2015 budget requests $506.3 million for global climate change related activities supported by State and USAID, a 10-percent increase over the fiscal year 2013 level.

Question. Given the increasing need for humanitarian assistance, democracy promotion, and embassy security measures, why is $506.3 million for global climate change the best expenditure of taxpayer funds?

Answer. As Secretary Kerry noted in the 2015 Congressional Budget Justification, we view climate-change investments as a smart way to promote stability and global prosperity, while protecting development gains that support economic growth, reduce climate-related security risks, and protect U.S. interests.

The proposed fiscal year 2015 $506.3 million is a combined Department of State-USAID request, with USAID requesting $348 million of that total. State Department and USAID climate change assistance will help countries reduce emissions and adapt to climate change, and will support U.S. diplomatic efforts to negotiate a new international climate agreement in 2015. U.S. leadership is particularly necessary at this time to forge partnerships to safeguard future generations from the dangerous and costly repercussions of global climate change.

U.S. investments in clean energy and sustainable landscapes help developing countries lower emissions. No country is isolated from the effects of climate change and developing countries are increasingly a source of greenhouse gas emissions; they likely already emit more than developed countries. A recently released report by the Council on Environmental Quality [1] finds that an additional one degree of warming beyond 2 degrees Celsius above preindustrial levels could result in an annual loss of 0.9 percent of global economic output. As just one example of potential consequences due to climate change, scientific analyses described in the recent National Climate Assessment and a 2011 National Research Council report have found that the areal extent of forest fires in the Western United States would increase dramatically—by a factor of four or more in some areas—relative to the recent past under relatively modest warming scenarios.[2] The National Climate Assessment also describes other impacts to the United States, including sea level rise and changes in precipitation due to climate change. By helping developing countries reduce their greenhouse gas emissions, we reduce long-term risk to the United States.

U.S. investments in adaptation improve resiliency to climate change and help to reduce the severity of future humanitarian disasters. For example, as noted in my testimony, USAID, in separate collaborations with NASA and the U.S. Army Corps of Engineers, is helping Bangladesh adopt a new flood forecasting system and ensure that storm shelters are built appropriately. In Ethiopia, we are supporting a range of activities—from drought warning systems to building water storage—to protect against future shortages in rainfall. These are prudent measures to reduce the damage of future disasters. Such disasters are anticipated to grow as precipitation patterns change and sea levels rise in line with current climate projections.

Question. Since 2010, how much funding has USAID spent on international climate change programs?

Answer. From FY 2010 to FY 2013, Congress has appropriated, and USAID has programmed, $1.386 billion for the Global Climate Change Initiative at USAID.

Question. What percentage of USAID's programs involve global climate change initiatives?

Answer. The Global Climate Change Initiative represents 2 percent of the $14.4 billion managed by USAID in FY 2013.

Reporting

Most aid programs are not evaluated to determine the actual impact of the assistance. Congress as well as the American people cannot determine whether taxpayer dollars are being used wisely when it is unclear if it succeeded or failed.

USAID's ability to demonstrate results through performance management and reporting was one of the most significant challenges identified by the Inspector General. The Inspector General's FY 2013 Annual Management Challenge statement said,

"Quality, reliability, and sufficiency of program data are essential to assess whether projects are making adequate progress and having the intended impact."

"Even though USAID has extensive guidance to help manage projects, accurate and supported results continues to be problematic."

---

[1] The Cost of Delaying Action to Stem Climate Change, July 2014.

[2] Melillo, Jerry M., Terese (T.C.) Richmond, and Gary W. Yohe, Eds., 2014: Climate Change Impacts in the United States: The Third National Climate Assessment. U.S. Global Change Research Program, 841 pp. doi:10.7930/J0Z31WJ2. National Research Council. Climate Stabilization Targets: Emissions, Concentrations, and Impacts over Decades to Millennia. Washington, DC: The National Academies Press, 2011.

Question. What percentage of USAID's international climate change programs had completed impact evaluations?

Answer. With the release of the Agency's Evaluation Policy in January 2011, USAID made an ambitious commitment to conduct quality program evaluation—the systematic collection and analysis of information and evidence about program performance and impact. Under the Evaluation Policy, missions are expected to evaluate their larger programs across all development areas.

In addition, USAID's Climate Change and Development Strategy, released in January 2012, called for the development of a learning agenda, which includes impact evaluations. Impact evaluations are based on models of cause and effect, and require a credible and rigorously defined counterfactual to control for factors other than the program activity that might account for the observed change. The first impact evaluation will be complete in early 2016.

Impact evaluations are rigorous and are conducted in parallel with program activities they are evaluating; they take a long time, are work-intensive, and are quite expensive. Therefore, only a small percentage of climate change programs—those that are best suited to help USAID answer key questions about development effectiveness—will be studied in this fashion.

Performance evaluations, on the other hand, while often incorporating before-after comparisons, are less involved and more affordable. A number of mid-term and final performance evaluations of USAID's climate change program activities have been completed. Examples include a midterm-evaluation of Ecuador's Sustainable Coasts and Forests Project and an end-of-project evaluation of the Philippines' Alliance for Mindanao Off-Grid Renewable Energy.

Question. Have those evaluations been made available to Congress and the public?

Answer. Yes. To facilitate sharing of evaluation findings, evaluation reports must be submitted to USAID's central document repository, the Development Experience Clearinghouse (https://dec.usaid.gov) within 3 months of the evaluation's conclusion.

Question. What is the timeline for the completion of all of the reviews assessing whether the international climate change projects are meeting their goals and are having the intended impact?

Answer. The review of USAID climate change projects is an on-going process that incorporates findings from both project monitoring and evaluation. Performance monitoring indicates whether desired results are occurring and whether project outcomes are on-track while performance and impact evaluations help determine if a project resulted in the intended outcomes. All USAID projects undergo performance monitoring and results are reported annually. In addition, a number of performance evaluations have been completed, and the first impact evaluation will be complete in early 2016.

Question. Why should Congress and the American people believe the results on international climate change programs, when the Inspector General has stated that USAID's inability to obtain accurate and supported results is a significant challenge?

Answer. With the release of USAID's Evaluation Policy and under USAID Forward, the Agency has reinforced its emphasis on quality monitoring and evaluation (M&E). We are continually working to improve M&E capacity as it relates to climate change initiatives. For instance, we have developed carbon calculators to facilitate systematic and comparable reporting on greenhouse gas reductions through USAID investments. As another example, we offer an M&E class tailored for climate change projects several times a year to improve performance monitoring and reporting by missions and their implementers. Moreover, we are currently updating global climate change standard indicators to better capture the results of our programs. In this process, we are working with donors and other practitioners to standardize performance measures, where feasible, and to share lessons learned on monitoring the performance of climate change assistance.

STUDY BY JEFF KUETER, PRESIDENT OF THE GEORGE MARSHALL INSTITUTE,
SUBMITTED BY SENATOR JOHN BARRASSO

May 2012

Is Climate a National Security Problem?

Jeff Kueter
President, George C. Marshall Institute

On May 3, Defense Secretary Leon Panetta told the Environmental Defense Fund that "the area of climate change has a dramatic impact on national security" because the various purported impacts of a warming climate "all raise demand for humanitarian assistance and disaster relief." According to the Defense Department's press account ("Panetta: Environment Emerges as National Security Concern," *American Forces Press Service*, May 3, 2012), the Secretary then called for ratification of the Law of the Sea Treaty and discussed the military's concerns about fuel costs.

The linkage between climate change and U.S. national security concerns is tenuous. While the Defense Department has significant interests in examining its use of energy, those concerns are not related to the climate-conflict hypothesis. Energy is expensive, requires a complicated supply and logistics operation, and puts men and women in harm's way as fuel convoys move through hostile environments. None of those concerns are related to climate change and any steps the military may take in this area will (or, at least, ought to be) judged on the merits of their contribution to military missions. No reasonable or unreasonable case can be made for DOD energy consumption being anything more than a trivial contributor to anthropogenic climate effects.

But, the linkage between "rising sea levels, severe droughts, the melting of the polar caps, the more frequent and devastating natural disasters" and increasing demand for U.S. disaster and humanitarian operations cited by Secretary Panetta rests on little more than conjecture and speculation. Predicting the future in a way that is meaningful for preparing strategy, budgets, programs or the composition and character of the nation's armed forces is challenging enough in those areas where defense planners have great experience and deep understanding. Projecting the assumed effects of human-induced climate change is imprecise. Climate forecasting rests on a mountain of assumptions about how the natural climate operates, how climatic variables interact with each other, how those interactions are best mathematically represented in a climate model, and whether there is adequate data to measure the variables. The climate models used to forecast the future fail to deliver (and may be incapable of producing) useful predictions at the regional level, which is the frame of analysis most pertinent to defense and security planning.

The Marshall Institute — Science for Better Public Policy

1601 North Kent Street, Suite 802 • Arlington, VA 22209
Phone (571) 970-3180 • Email: info@marshall.org • Website: www.marshall.org

The depictions of the future that are used are consequently highly uncertain, but uniformly suggestive of terrible environmental outcomes. To complete the climate-security argument, the intelligence community and various think tanks have asked retired generals and admirals, intelligence analysts, and other national security scholars to uncritically accepted those conclusions about the environment and deliver assessments of what the world would be like should such scenarios unfold. To no great surprise, the conclusions about the security implications also are negative.

None of the climatological phenomena mentioned by Secretary Panetta directly impact U.S. security. They have to cause something else to happen and whatever that is (usually refugees or state instability) has to be substantial enough to warrant a response by the U.S. The empirical studies done on the subject suggest strongly that neither environmental stresses nor refugees are significant sources of international conflict. For example, three Norwegian scholars recently examined the linkage between drought and the onset of conflict for *International Security*, a preeminent security studies journal. They found "little scientific evidence" in support of the claims and noted that "there is no direct, short-term relationship between drought and civil war onset, even within contests presumed most conducive to violence."

Examining the climate wars argument in the *Washington Quarterly*, Dr. Bruno Tertrais of the Foundation for Strategic Research notes:

> "History shows that "warm" periods are more peaceful than "cold" ones. In the modern era, the evolution of the climate is not an essential factor to explain collective violence. Nothing indicates that "water wars" or floods of "climate refugees" are on the horizon. And to claim that climate change may have an impact on security is to state the obvious – but it does make it meaningful for defense planning."

The natural variability of climate guarantees there will be droughts, storms, and natural disasters. Individuals, nations, and international organizations ought to rightly prepare to meet those challenges as they are clearly knowable. In doing so, they prepare as well for whatever impact may arise from human-induced climate change, particularly on the time-scale relevant to defense budgeting, force planning, and development of strategic thought. Further, as Joshua Busby rightly notes, "a modest investment in risk reduction and adaptation in poor countries will likely be much more cost-effective and security enhancing than responding to humanitarian disasters through military and relief operations."

If there is no empirical basis to believe that climate causes conflict, what is it that Secretary Panetta would have the U.S. prepare to address? The answer, as Busby implies, is greater use of the American military as the world's FEMA or Red Cross. The assumption Secretary Panetta asks the public to accept, and he is not along in doing so, is that there is a moral obligation on the part of the United States to "help" those harmed or displaced around the world. Without question the U.S. is a philanthropic nation, quick and generous to aid those in distress. Over the years, the U.S. military, by virtue of its logistical acumen and available resources and manpower, has become the lead agent in government for responding to these crises. In a world where hypothetically these humanitarian crises are more frequent, the assumption is that the U.S. and its military will be ever more engaged.

That is not necessarily so, of course. The United States does not respond now to every humanitarian crisis and these types of operations are a relatively new occurrence, enabled by fast transportation abilities and responsive logistics systems. We, as a nation, elected to assume this role for ourselves and one can imagine a time when we might redefine our national interests more narrowly. In a world where there are more humanitarian crises, or we are more aware of them, just such a redefinition of roles and interests is likely, if for no other reason than resource constraints.

In short, the United States faces many security challenges in the months and years ahead – environmentally induced conflict ranks low amongst them.